Dear Ste

You're Going Deaf

THANK You!

Steven Louis DiCesare

ACKNOWLEDGMENTS

Special thanks to my editor and brainstorming partner, Jill Bielawski.
And to Carla, Bob, Josh, Mike, and Tracey, who took the time to read the
manuscript and provide meaningful and honest feedback.
To Ian Miller for providing images, vitality and soul to my stories.
To Mark and all my friends, some of whose names I might have changed,
but who might recognize their roles in these stories.
And deep gratitude to my family and especially my wife, Tracey,
for her patience, understanding and support.
Without them, these stories would have no meaning.

Contents

August 1, 2014, 3:07 a.m.

Dear Steve,

OK man, that's enough. Get out of the basement—right now. Go to the bathroom and look at yourself. Look at the man in the glass and tell him to go outside. Tell him to remember what his father told him. Right now! Go. Get up. Tell him to get out of there for his family upstairs. Tell him he's weathered worse things and he's going to get through this too. I don't care if it's the middle of the night. Go take a walk. Come on, man. You got this! Tuesday night was way worse. Why don't you go take a walk around the block and then make some tea? You're going to get through this one, just like you got through the last one. Steve, you are going to be OK. How about some push-ups or even another episode of Gilmore Girls? Do those damn meditation exercises that doctor suggested. Come on man, do *something*.

You can do it!

Hang on, buddy,
Steve

Audiologist Report   **1969 – 1979, Birth – Age 10**

<u>Hearing Status</u>: Hearing at birth. No evidence of hearing loss until age 10.

<u>Hyperacusis</u> (sensitivity to specific sounds): No evidence of hyperacusis.

<u>Tinnitus</u>: No documented tinnitus.

<u>Notes</u>: Two-parent household in a middle-to-upper-class community. Normal to high exposure to language and communication.

I was born hearing, as was my older brother by two years. There was no documentation or evidence of hearing problems in my family. My mom was tuned in to all the modern trends in education and language development. We attended preschools, Montessori schools and kindergarten extension programs, and had lots of opportunities for social play in the community. I developed language at a normal rate and showed no evidence of hearing impairments until the age of 9 or 10. Even now, many people I meet as a Deaf adult remark on my speech clarity: "No way! I might not have even known you are Deaf! I just kind of thought you were British or Australian." "You're Deaf? Wow! You speak really well for a Deaf person."

I attribute this semi-clear speech to the strong language base I had for those hearing years and the slow decline of the loss. I had 10 or so years of normal language development, with five or so more years of exposure to language with partial hearing. I was very lucky to have that. A person born Deaf, with the percentage of hearing loss that I have now, would not be understood without many hours of speech therapy and training, or possibly, at all.

Audiologist Report   **1980 – 1989, Age 10 – 20**

<u>Hearing Status</u>: Gradual decline, mild to moderate hearing loss. Bilateral, sensorineural. Approximately 65 percent loss at age 20.

<u>Hyperacusis</u>: Mild to moderate sensitivity to loud, sharp sounds.

<u>Tinnitus</u>: Tinnitus establishing itself as a high-pitched white noise at about 30 percent blanket over the residual hearing.

<u>Notes</u>: Not using hearing aids. Not using preferential seating in classes. Overuse of hearing protection due to hyperacusis in the form of foam earplugs and construction-grade earmuffs.

Good Morning, My Friend

I am 10 years old and I wake up one morning. It's a Saturday or Sunday. I know this because my dad is still in the house. I can hear, or maybe just feel, his heavy footsteps walking around downstairs. If it were a weekday, he would be at work by the time I got up.

I wake up this weekend morning and am rolling around in bed, wondering what that sound is. I have my own room at this point and plenty of time to mull it over. *Sounds like a buzzing something or other, maybe the heater … the water running through the heater?* I get out of bed to get closer to the heater unit and put my ear right up against it. No change. Not the heater. While I'm down on all fours, I crawl around my room, toward the window. *Sounds like some buzzing or hissing with some chirps and crackles. Maybe something is going on outside?* I open the window and stick my head against the screen. No change. *Hmmm…. The toilet is running?* I go into the bathroom that joins my room with my brother's. No change. Must be something downstairs. I head to the steps and take them two at a time until the bottom, where I go for the final four in one jump. I go through the living room and further investigate for the source of the buzzing, hissing, chirping noise. It's probably coming from the kitchen. But the dishwasher is not running, nor is the sink faucet. *Maybe it's the fridge motors and the cooling and freezing engine gadget thingy?* I go and stick my ear on the fridge. No change. Standing there in my jammies, in the kitchen, next to the fridge, it started to dawn on me. I stuck my fingers in my ears. No change. Took them out. No change. Put them back in. No change. I go looking for my mom and find her in the den folding clothes.

"Mom, there's a noise in my head," I say, and go downstairs to the basement to practice for my piano lesson in the afternoon.

March 14, 2014, 2:40 a.m.

Dear Steve,

You've got to remember that little guy. Do you remember him? Not a care in the world! What can you learn from Young Stevie that could help you right now, to get through this crap you're dealing with? What is that little guy telling you?

Yes, man! Yes! You've got to live like the little kids, man! Little kids are in the moment. Little kids are concerned with the NOW. Little kids aren't too worried about what's going to happen tomorrow or what happened yesterday. If they made a mistake yesterday, well, that's gone. Move on and try again. Yesterday is like a lifetime ago to little kids. They're not worried or concerned about what might happen to them tomorrow like adults are, because right NOW is where it's at! Right NOW is the good stuff! If they're not starving right NOW, if they're not too cold or too hot right NOW, they are all right. They are creating, imagining, playing, exploring and being in the NOW.

Steve! You need to be more like that little guy; be in the NOW. Young Stevie wasn't too worried about what was going to happen to his hearing that day. He didn't keep focusing on what caused the noise in his head that day. It was a little weird and a little strange, but Young Stevie accepted that it was what it was and kept living in the NOW! He had stuff to do—today! He had places to go, castles to storm and planets to explore. He could deal with some noises in his head. He would make those noises his new little friends. No problem.

You can do it,
Steve

The Fireman's Fair

I've been putting together bands and music recording projects forever. I remember one time, when I was 12 years old, going to my town's Fireman's Fair a few blocks from my house with my brother and neighbors. There were all the usual town fair events, games and booths.

At the end of the night, on the way out, before going home, you get a "grab bag." You put your hand in one of four holes and grab a bag of kid stuff. So that one year, I got a bag filled with little plastic rock band stuff! A guitar, a sax, a mini drum set, a mic … that kind of thing. So, walking home, under a streetlight, we checked it all out. I was psyched! I remember hanging out there for hours while we handed out instruments and "rocked out." I organized a little song with an intro, some lyrics, a guitar solo, drum solo and head-banging ending. We even named the group after something from an arcade video game that was just released. We called our group something along the lines of "Gamelon's Fart Mania" and went home to perform for my parents. My first band! Fart Mania. Funny what I remember. I clearly remember each and every band, recording, music project, engineer, studio personnel and musician I've played with since then.

There was another memorable aspect of the Fireman's Fair. To signal the beginning of the fair, they would run the firehouse siren at 6 p.m. We always waited near my house for the siren to go off, and I would always hold my ears. My neighbors wouldn't. My brother would. Sometimes we would be too excited to go and start walking over, but after age 10, I would never go into the fairgrounds before 6. I always waited a block or two away for the siren to go off, and held my ears.

My first band and my first warning.

May 21, 2014, 3:07 a.m.

Dear Steve! Stevie! Steverino! Steveroni!

Don't forget little Stevie's dreams and fantasies. His wonderment about creating new things, building things, imagining. Don't let your disabilities or fears limit you! Don't let them keep you from trying new things, creating new visions. You have to continue to take some chances and follow those crazy fantasies that pop into your head but dissipate because they seem immature or unattainable.

There will be voices working against you. Watch out! "You're going to fail" or "You're not good enough to do that!" or "All that work and you're going to suck." Or "All that work and nobody's going to like it" or "You suck at following through on new stuff!" or "You just suck; you're a loser!" These are the noisy voices. Steve! Do not listen to these voices. Tell these voices to take a hike. "Go to hell, you noisy bastards!"

Somewhere in there is the quiet voice. The "*hey*" voice, ready with a genuine idea and waiting for you to notice. Don't let those noisy bastards hold you back from connecting with the *hey* voice. Do not dismiss the quiet voice, the one that says, "*Hey*, wouldn't it be cool to put a band together and play on that corner at the mall?" Or "*Hey*! Wouldn't it be neat to start your own consulting business?" "*Hey*, you really want to ice-dance! Wouldn't it be great if I could learn to ice-dance and skate out on the lake?" "*Hey*, wouldn't it be great to spend more time playing with the kids, just lie on the floor with the kids for an hour every day? *Hey*, wouldn't that be awesome?"

Come on, Steve! You hear those *hey* voices all the time. You know them pretty well. Just last week you heard one suggest, "*Hey*, wouldn't it be cool to learn how to make 3-D animation and make a short movie? You could put some of your music on there! That would be awesome!" Remember that voice? You heard it, and you remember it. What are you going to do about it? What's been going on recently that's holding you back?

With love,
Steve

Stata-Ten

Thus began the many trips to the doctors. Through my teens, trips to the doctor leveled out to every six months or so for data collection and to see if there were any new treatments for my hearing loss. Most of the time, my mom would bring me to the doctors, but once in a while, my dad would take me. I would look forward to these trips, because other than just being different from the common Mom Trip, with Dad Trips, there was always a sandwich involved. Usually we would order a meatball or chicken parmesan sub at the bar in a small Italian restaurant or diner geared toward the blue-collar lunch crowd that permeates the community we lived in.

I remember one trip to the doctor's found me waiting for my dad by the windows in the middle school office, watching him get out of his pickup truck in his late 1970s suit, those brown and tan ones with the elbow patches. My dad had a kind of blue-collar turned white-collar job—the kind that wears the suit and tie but still gets hands-on time in the job. So the suit probably felt kind of awkward for him and looked kind of awkward to others, but in my retrospective mind, with the 70s cut and colors on it, it was just very cool.

We arrive at the doctor's office and do the audiogram tests. I am in the booth for a while looking through the thick military-grade glass at the audiologist and my dad, raising my hands in response to the beeps. Repeating those two-syllable words and entertaining myself with middle school silliness, such as repeating "Batman" every time the audiologist asks a question.

"Say *baseball*," he prompts.

"Batman?" I say.

"Say *ice cream*."

"Batman." Smirk.

"Say *cowboy*." He smiles.

"Batman. Just kidding. Cowboy?"

We finish the tests and go meet with the audiologist and the MD. This is the part where my parents try to follow the updates and forecast for my hearing future. They make me sit on my hands so as not to irritate everyone with my incessant tapping and drumming on chairs and tables.

The results are always the same. I remember these results always being spoken to my parents, almost as if I weren't there. Looking back, I guess it was just the norm of the times to address the parent, and maybe that professional manner was because they weren't sure if I was hearing or understanding all the info. But this visit went something like this: "Your son lost some more hearing … and some decibels in the midrange … voice recognition will be … blah blah blah.… Qualified as a 'moderate–severe hearing loss' … blah blah," says the doctor.

My dad is listening and conversing with them about it. We knew what to expect, but I think this visit showed a more aggressive jump in my hearing loss.

The doctor is trying to scramble some positives into it: "You know, Steve is going to be fine because he's very good-looking. He is a very good-looking boy, and he is just going to be fine. Oftentimes, I see patients with a similar pathology, and they really rise up and excel in face of the loss. I see those qualities in Steve."

"Batman," I say.

This was not the only time a doctor told me I was going to be OK with the deafness because I was good-looking. I was told this three times in my life by three different doctors. Is this a strategy they teach in medical school? Regardless, it worked. I remember what that doctor said, especially about rising up in face of the loss. It seemed like a challenge.

We went out to the truck, and I remember sitting there feeling a little scared that I was losing more hearing and feeling a little like Batman because I was so "good-looking." I could tell my dad was a little wrought up over the visit. He was not a very talkative guy, kind of quiet and to the point, with much wisdom in short sentences.

"Hey Steve, you're going to get through this. Stata-ten, you understand?"

"Yeah," I answered, and we went to get a sandwich.

"Stata-ten" is derivation of an Italian phrase that my father grew up with as a kid in an Italian-speaking household in an Italian neighborhood in the Bronx. I recently found out that it's a dialectal interpretation of the phrase "Stati attenti," which translates to something like, "Watch what you're doing." I just accepted it as a blanket term for different situations. It always seemed to work, and I always understood. "Do the right thing," "Pay attention," "Be careful," "Don't embarrass your family," "Focus." Stata-ten.

May 2, 2014, 2:14 a.m

Dear Steve,

That's about all you need to know, right there in one Italian mini-phrase, "Stata-ten." Listen to your father. Remember what he said. Pay attention to what you're doing when you're doing it. Stata-ten. Do one thing at a time and stay focused. Keep your focus and you will succeed; you will get through it. Stata-ten. Focus on your family. Take care of the family, elder and younger. It's not just you, Steve; you represent many others. Don't do anything to embarrass the family name. Stata-ten. Do the right thing, always, even when nobody's looking, and do it with pride. Be careful. Slow down and do it right. Stata-ten.

With a "love tap" upside the back of the head,
Steve

Fast Eddie

The doctors and audiologists all had the same conclusion, so we were pretty much settled on a diagnosis. "Your son has a mild-to-moderate, bilateral, sensorineural hearing loss, which is commonly accompanied by tinnitus sounds. Hearing aids would be a good idea at this time to keep language acquisition at an optimal level. It is possible that we will see more loss, so be prepared for that. You are encouraged to bring in your other son for testing, as this looks to be a genetic disorder."

Anytime I went to these appointments with my parents, the doctors continued to address them as if I weren't there. Not until I started going to appointments alone would the doctors address me directly. Even later, when I started going to appointments as an adult with another adult such as my wife, or even with my children, oftentimes the doctors would address my wife or kids to relay the info to me.

My brother began the assessments and was diagnosed with the same exact type of loss I had, but it was just starting to show itself when I was eleven. He is a few years older, yet the decline in my hearing initiated at a younger age.

In the town where I grew up, a suburb of New York City, there were no visible role models for people with disabilities. I don't think that "mainstreaming" in the schools was happening yet. So, the hearing aid idea was pretty much shot down by this 12-year-old. There were no visually obvious students with disabilities in my school. There were no students in wheelchairs. There were no kids with hearing aids, and I didn't want to break that ground.

At one point, there actually had been a kid with giant hearing aids in my school. He walked really fast, and sometimes he was in a wheelchair, wheeling really fast. He had a humongous overflowing backpack, his head was constantly tilted to one side, and he really cruised through the halls. His name was Eddie, and everyone called him Fast Eddie. He got teased a lot, and there were a lot of "Fast Eddie" jokes that year. He attended our school for less than a year before moving on to what was hopefully a better situation.

My mom asks, "Steven, do you want to try some hearing aids?"

"Nah."

"The doctors really think it'll help you stay on top of things in class," she says in a doctor voice.

"Nah."

"Well the doctors think it might block out some of the hissing noises. You know? Like pushing them aside. We should try it!"

"No."

"It might help with your music too. You'll be able to really hear the high notes on the piano. Let's get them, and if you don't like them, you don't have to wear them," she tries.

"Nah," I reply, thinking about Fast Eddie.

March 22, 2014, 1:35 a.m.

Dear Steve,

Hey! C'mon, man! You couldn't try the hearing aids? You were worried about what your friends in middle school would think, weren't you? You were worried about being teased. Listen, man, little Stevie wouldn't have cared what people thought about his hearing aids. He probably would've thought they were cool like the bionic man. Cool like an astronaut. He wouldn't have been concerned about what people thought of him tomorrow, and if they teased him today, he might have just laughed along with them and kept playing. Your mom was right. Maybe hearing aids would have helped. You should have listened to your mother.

Love,
Steve

Day Camp

"Molly Jones? You're with Tomahawk-12," yells the camp director.

"Anthony Leoni! Eagle-14." The director is calling off all the kids' names and which group they are to report to.

It's the summer of 1981. I am turning 12 later this summer, and my brother, Chris, is 14. We are sitting in this giant lodge with about 100 other kids we don't know. This is a weeklong day camp down in the neighboring town on the bay that we didn't really want to go to, but Mom forced us to. It's the usual summer camp stuff, sports and swimming with a Native American theme, as is a lot of stuff in the region where we grew up.

Man, why can't they come up with a better system than this? Calling off individual names? C'mon! Then you have to get up in front of everyone and walk all the way across the hall to your group leader in front of everyone. C'mon, guys! It's 1981! Can't we do something with names on color-coded cards or something at the door? It would save, like, 20 minutes, too!

Chris and I are sitting there on the floor with all the other kids, and I am asking him after every name that's called if it was me. I'm not able to make out names through the noises in the lodge. "Was that me?" He's telling me to shush. "Was that me?" He's got a hearing loss too and he's struggling to hear the guy. "Was that us?" Shush! It's filtering down to about 15 kids and we are still sitting there. All the groups are gathered along the walls of the room, and individual group leaders are welcoming everyone and bonding their group with high-fives and stuff. It's getting louder, and we are now sitting there with just eight kids and the director is still calling off names.

We are the last of three as the groups head out to their activities. *Why weren't we called? Did we miss it, or are we not registered or something?* Chris gets up and motions me to follow him over to the camp director. There's another kid already there, and the director checks his chart and tells the kid where to go, and she sprints to catch up with her group. Chris is checking in with the guy and I am cursing my mom for making us do this camp. The hall is pretty cleared out now; all the groups have headed out to their various activity areas. My brother spells our names to the guy and he says he called us already; he's been doing it alphabetically. Chris gets his instructions and group name. The guy looks at me and tells me that I'm in Tomahawk-12 and "Looks like they headed out to the softball field for Round 1. So, go out that door, around Shmerkwin Hall, then go *flerpity skoo-napper* and follow that trail to the fields. Have a great day, campers! Go Hawks, Go Eagles!"

I follow my brother to the doors. We are both totally not into this and pretty mad at my mom. He waves and jogs over to meet up with his group. I start looking for Shmerkwin Hall. *What's a Shmerkwin? Is that an Indian name?* There are like three big buildings in front of me and I can't seem to find any identification markings. I walk forward, past a building that says "Algonquin." *What'd he say? Go down a trail to the fields?* There's a bunch of routes to choose from, and I pick one and it turns into a footpath through trees and bushes and then opens up to a big field. There are four or five groups out here, and I walk around a bit but nobody says anything. I head out past the groups, through the field, trying to be cool. I keep walking toward the tree line, trying hard to not start crying. I am planning to hide in the trees.

As I pass the archery range area, someone grabs my shoulder. It's Chris. He knows what's up. He waves me back to the fields and I follow him down. He points to a group and I run down there. I ask if this is Tomahawk-12 and the group leaders say, "Yeah! Can you play third base? Nobody wants to. Here, use this glove." I run out to third and it seems like everyone is staring at me.

OK. Sports. Cool. My brother and I and the kids on our block play sports and games on our street and in our driveway all summer and after school every day. We've played every single sport, every organized game, as well as made up sports such as "Combat Basketball"' and "Over the House Tennis." I am pretty good at sports and games, and the rest of the week at camp goes OK as I get over missing the introductions and everybody's names and just blend in with the activities. I'm still kind of mad at my mom though.

May 18, 2014, 1:26 a.m.

Dear Steve,

Hey man, I know that particular day camp experience started a little rough, but think about all those times your mom got you into those cool camps! The science camps! Remember those? You guys spent a week every summer making rockets and doing science projects. The woodburning and woodcarving workshops? What about all those art camps? Those were great! You consider yourself a bit of an artist, right? You have a degree to teach art, no? Well, your mom started you on that degree program when you were like 6 years old, Steve! All those art workshops in the back of the local hobby shop, the science camps, the music camps and music lessons! Ha ha! Your mom helped make you the artist you are today, man! You had a very caring mom who gave her all and tried to expose you to the best and varied experiences.

Go Hawks!
Steve

Sleepaway Camp

1984. I am turning 15 this summer and it's my last year of three, going to Boy Scout summer camp. I am going to hit Eagle Scout this coming year, and I'll be doing teen stuff and working full-time next summer. This is a two-week sleepaway camp for scouts from all over the state. I attend with my troop, which is very strong and large and has a lot of parent support. My dad has been scoutmaster for the past two years, and other fathers whom I grew up with have been scoutmasters and leaders for our troop. My dad was here this summer for one of the weeks, and my brother was getting paid as a camp counselor.

We spend two weeks working on merit badges during the day for camping, wilderness survival, first aid, swimming and citizenship. Then, nights and weekends were for activities with friends and free time. I loved the free time we had to create our own activities. I used the time to learn and improve sculptural woodcarving, making plaques for our troop's submission for the main wall at the lodge, and practicing the guitar.

I also spent a lot of time putting together various performance groups. We'd perform original written skits, circus-type acts, and songs around our nightly campfires in our troop's social area, inside the circle of 20 or so platform tents. Once a week on Friday evening, the entire camp, about 12 troops, would hike out to the gorge where there would be some sort of scouting ceremony, and then each troop could sign up to perform at the big campfire. Yeah! I signed up every time they allowed me to.

Our final performance at the gorge at scout camp consisted of our troop's "rock" band. I went to the mess hall and borrowed white uniforms and a bunch of empty Heinz vinegar bottles. I made the guys wear these uniforms so we would all have the same white clothes on. I always had my guitar at summer camp and campouts. So, I would play guitar, another boy would play sticks,

26

another on harmonica, another would sing, and one boy played the Heinz bottles filled with water tuned to four or five different tones. I can still remember just about where to fill a Heinz vinegar bottle to get an A, D and C tone. We opened with one of my junky blues originals, which didn't go over too well with the campers. Then we closed with *Stairway to Heaven,* which we'd worked on for two weeks, every night. It got a standing ovation, mostly because of the awesome singing from my scout friend who is also in the school choir.

The daytime merit badge work was organized in classroom format. So, for example, Camping Merit Badge class would be conducted by an older scout counselor like my brother, and there would be about 15 younger scouts working toward earning the merit badge.

These classes, during camp this year, were the first time I grew aware that I was missing "important stuff" because of my hearing loss, and were unfortunately where I developed destructive habits around classrooms and classwork.

I was sitting there, realizing I was missing stuff, but I wouldn't advocate for myself or go to the front of the group to read lips more easily. I wouldn't ask for clarification, ask questions or volunteer. I would stay in the back or on the side with my friends and act cool. I'd get the info later, somehow.

This was denial. A challenge against the hearing loss. Steve versus the slow, creeping forces of evil. A way of fighting back and having some control. *You are taking my hearing. My communication. My music. Fuck You!*

I continued this denial through high school, where I wouldn't even sit in the first three rows of any class, accept any special education assistance, try hearing aids or ask the teacher for notes. You can't lip-read and write notes at the same time. I continued the denial through five years of university classes in giant lecture halls with 300-plus students, and in small classrooms with 30 students. I continued it through my 20s as we took the band out to do shows and record albums.

I continued this denial, in some respects, right up to the current day, because to accept the fact that I was going deaf would be to accept the fact that I can't make music. Oil and water. They just don't mix. *"Do not go gentle into that good night ... Rage, rage against the dying of the light." Fuck! You!*

May 17, 2014, 3:03 a.m.

Dear Steve,

Acceptance is the only way. You know this. I'm not saying to give up, but does acceptance have to mean letting go? Can you fully accept the situation, any situation, and then channel some of that fight energy to persevere? Acceptance to persevere!

"On my honor I will do my best to do my duty … to keep myself physically strong, mentally awake and morally straight." Good stuff! "A scout is trustworthy, loyal, helpful, friendly, courteous, kind, obedient…." Good stuff, man!

They really got it all in there. Kinda "Leave it to Beaver" corny but the foundations of EVERYTHING are in there. You really need to look back over that Scout Law and Oath stuff. Then do it again.

You are lucky to have had the scouting experience with your brother and dad, Steve. You learned a lot of good stuff through that troop. You know what was the most important? Realizing that the parents built that troop and made it great. Realizing that the community offered time and support for you kids and how important that is for any kid. Your dad was a scoutmaster, man! He helped you become the youngest Eagle Scout in the troop! Those were awesome days, and he taught you guys a lot without you even knowing it. Isn't that how you approach your profession as an educator now? Your dad let you guys create and be kids, be idiots and be extraordinary, and he never let any BS through. "Do the right thing," he always said. You were really lucky to have supportive people around while you were young. Do you recognize that?

Boy Scout Salute,
Steve

Art Skyd

Like a Rhinestone Cowboy, F-chord to C-chord. C-chord-C-chord on a horse in a Cmaj7 Rodeooo, Oh! Oooh! ... I can't do this down here! Creepy! By the seventh grade, I flat-out refused to play the piano anymore. Our basement, where the piano was kept, was dark, humid and full of monsters. They hung out behind the bar in the back corner, and I just couldn't play down there anymore, with them creeping out and joining in on the choruses.

My mom suggested I take up guitar like my brother had. I liked this idea because the guitar seemed cooler, and I'd recently made a friend, Mark at school who played guitar. I took some lessons and started to really connect with the instrument. By eighth grade, I was ready to start a real rock-and-roll band, and I shot the idea to Mark. He was totally on board, and we started rehearsing and writing. Mark and I became good buddies, and he turned out to be a lifelong partner in crime. In high school we decided to name our band, flipped a coin to see who would get to play bass, found a drummer and named the band *Art Skyd*. Spelled backward, it's the last name of a famous baseball player on the Mets, Lenny Dykstra. We practiced a lot and played at dances and parties all through high school.

Through these formative years, Mark and I began the process of accommodating our environment in the jam space to counter the effects of my hearing loss. We experimented with different amp arrangements, couch cushions, pillows, blankets and sound-blocking barriers. We built folding movable walls out of plexiglass that we could strategically position in the rehearsal room to optimize my hearing.

While we were playing more and more, my hearing was gradually declining. Was the music damaging my hearing? I knew there was a hearing loss, declining over the years since I first got tested at age 10. I knew I had the hyperacusis problem, being

31

sensitive to those high-pitched sounds. *Was playing music damaging my hearing?!* This is a tough thing to face as a teenager who identifies as a musician and who is creating, writing, performing and being adored by girls across all four grades in high school. I had many inner battles those years about my need to express myself through music and its possible damaging effects on my declining hearing.

I was lucky enough to have three things happen in the next few years that helped me keep writing and playing music. First, my mother was frantic about me wearing earplugs from the very first rehearsals through the present day. I'm in my 40s now, and she still surreptitiously checks if I have my earplugs in when we're in a loud environment with a band or at a festival. When we go out to dinner, she calls early and finagles with the restaurant staff to get us a table away from any loud kitchen noise, sometimes even in the private dining room in the back.

Second, my dad listened to my recordings. He wasn't a music person. But whenever I finished a recording, he would sit down in the living room with the old Walkman tape deck and headphones and listen to the whole thing. It's a funny picture in my head because he never listened to music outside of his truck, he never wore headphones and he never sat in the living room otherwise. But he did listen to all my final recordings and even made comments about them. "Steve, I liked that song 'Lester' — it had a nice rhythm." Also, the first couple of years when the band was trying to get serious about playing gigs in later high school, he came for an hour or so to almost every gig we did that was within reasonable driving range and would get him home by midnight.

The third thing was that my older brother has exactly the same issues I do with hearing loss, sensitivity and deafness. Our differences are social. He is somewhat reclusive and virtually always chooses a quiet environment. He is extremely skilled in many areas, and all of them are "quiet" activities. He is an accomplished guitarist too but plays mostly classical music and jazz. His hearing loss is progressing in exactly the same way mine is. So I realized that, logically, it seemed my hearing loss was going to progress regardless of my exposure to loud sounds. This was the crucial revelation that allowed me to continue writing, recording and performing.

August 13, 2014, 3:20 a.m.

Dear Steve,

You know what I see here, man? Stories of your family and how they supported you. Do not underestimate the foundation your family provided for you. You're lucky to have a supportive family and friends who continues to help you through life's transitions. Very lucky!

Hugs,
Steve

A Big Night

11:57 p.m. Time to boogie. *Let's do it, man.* I slip off the covers and drop my legs to the floor, slowly and quietly. I'm fully dressed except for my special sneakers, which are ready and waiting by my feet. They are not really special in any structural way, but I gave them special powers, like a good-luck charm. I put on my special sneakers, stand up slowly and put the blankets back, make my bed, and place the note in full view on top of the blankets.

I am 16 years old and a junior in high school. It's Friday night, and my parents are very strict. Earlier tonight, I was told to be home at 10:00, and I was home at 10:00. Not 10:01, not 10:02. I sprinted a few blocks to make it on time tonight, and all is well. I kissed my mom good night as she sniffed me thoroughly for scents of alcohol. I passed the "good-night kiss test," and my dad followed me upstairs a few minutes later to say good night. I gave my dad a kiss and he went back downstairs as I brushed my teeth. My brother was already in bed in his room across the hall. I turned off the lights and slipped into bed, fully clothed. Waiting.

11:57 p.m. The calculated time. This is the fifth or sixth time I've snuck out of the house at night. My room is on the second floor, right above my parent's bedroom. The first few attempts, I got out on the roof ledge outside my room and just jumped off, doing an amateur ninja-roll landing. This method was taking its toll on me physically and mentally. I started to realize what a risk it was. Feeling the pain from a 12-foot jump off the roof on the third mission, doing the roll and trying to limp-sprint back behind the big maple tree, I realized what I'd need to do if I broke my leg or cracked a rib at 1 in the morning — wake my parents up anyway with a trip to the emergency room. So I devised a new method of getting out of the house and down to ground-level safely without being heard or seen, and it proved successful in the first couple of trials.

11:58 p.m. From the bed, one big double step toward the window, a single step at about 10:30 on the left side, another single step toward the window, the big double step directly to the right side of the desk, hand to the wall for support, and then the single step around the desk and ahead to the window and the small table with the Fostex 4-track cassette recorder. Growing up in this room, I had this squeak-free pathway all mapped out years ago. I also had pathways to sneak up on my brother in his room, get to the bathroom or get to the top of the steps. Even with my hearing loss (approximately 60 percent at this time), it's still obvious by touch and feeling through my feet where to step and not to step. By age 16, I've perfected each pathway.

12:01 a.m. I power on the Fostex 4-track machine. I have a mic hooked up to it laying on an old shirt pointing toward the window. I am waiting for the train to come into the station in my town, about four lateral blocks away from my side of the house. It is scheduled for 12:02. I can usually feel it or sense the low rumble of the train, but with my hearing loss, I can't be certain I'm pinpointing the high-pitched horn. So I've set the mic up to the Fostex machine, which I tested numerous times, and I'm confident about how the LED input light on the machine signals the train horn.

12:02 a.m. I feel the train coming. Yes, it's definitely the train, it's coming, right on time. I watch the LED display on the Fostex with my hands on the window. Waiting … any second now. My heart is thumping! There is the first toot, all the way from low green to red on the display. As the second horn sounds and the display hits red, I slide the window up and breathe in the cool fresh air of freedom. Taking a minute to calm myself, and a few deep breaths, I take stock of the status in the house. All seems still. I'm totally in the zone as I climb out onto the roof ledge.

The ledge is a three-foot-wide sloped runner along the length of the house, protecting the main level with gutters. I shimmy across the ledge sideways, with my face to the house, grabbing indents and abnormalities in the shingle siding with my fingertips for balance. I sidestep past the bathroom separating my room and my brother's. Past my brother's room and over to the safety of the remodeled kitchen roof, which is an easy step onto the full 14x14 gently sloped roof of the kitchen. In later missions I sometimes went through my brother's room and out his window, which leads onto the kitchen roof. Somehow, I never woke him.

From the kitchen roof, I climb up the steeper garage roof to the front peak, over the basketball hoop. From the peak, I shimmy down and over the side to stand on the hoop itself, then spin sideways a bit and into a crouch. Inching my body over the hoop and finally hanging on the rim, I then drop the two or three feet to the driveway. My dad and I regularly reinforced the backboard and hoop with half-inch bolts into the garage wall, with nuts and locking washers, because the rattle of a loose backboard makes the whole neighborhood echo.

Let's do it, man! I'd left my bike on the side of the house yesterday. I walk it out through the yard to the front pine tree and wait and watch the house for a few minutes. One time while I was behind the big pine, lights came on in the kitchen, and I saw my dad checking things out. Our dog, Sparky, was probably barking at the faint creaks and crackles from someone walking across the roof. From the pine tree, I need to get through a full house lot length of street in front of my house, which is fully exposed by a streetlight. My dad could be standing by the living room window in the dark, watching. So I cross the street into Mr. Ray's yard and walk the bike in the shadows, behind the rows of trees he has lining the street. Final check back toward my house. Looks good. I mount my bike and head out of my small dead-end street to the main road and freedom.

Down toward the harbor and the bridge running over the dam. Up hills, down hills, up bigger hills and down bigger hills. *I'm on the ground, can't hear a sound and I'm hunting after you, (I'm lost?) and I'm found, (fooling?) around, and I'm hungry like the wolf.* I have that new Duran Duran song cycling in my head. I'm cruising now. My bike is tuned up, greased up and running smoothly. But this is no 3-speed mountain bike or 10-speed road bike. This is the old cruiser, back-pedal brakes, no-gear street bike. How I managed to ride this bike multiple times without a helmet for the 4-mile round trip, on a main road at night, without getting hurt, a flat tire or pulled over by the police, seems like a miracle.

Heart pumping up the hills, wind in my hair down the hills. Cruising. I arrive at the destination. A house in a quiet residential court in the neighboring town, across the bridge and on the other side of the harbor. I stash my bike next to the garage in the bushes and make my way around the back to the TV room. The TV is on, muted, and she is waiting by the window.

The window is the old side-open, hand-crank type that goes almost all the way perpendicular to the plane of the house. She is cranking confidently, and I figure she sprayed it earlier with the WD-40 that I found on the back of her dad's workbench in the garage. We've been dating for about a year now, and I've been in this house often. The window is wide open, and I climb in easily and brush away the heavy drapes covering the window.

"Hey Ba–". She stops my whisper with a kiss. We are making out within seconds, right in the middle of the TV room. Lots of tongue. French kissing was really a highlight of the makeout sessions back then. And hickeys in hidden places. I'm pulling my T-shirt off, then hers. We're on the floor and I'm on top. *Hell yeah!* I kick off my shoes and peel off my pants and throw them to the side. *Damn! I wore my tighty whities?!* We are back into deep-tongue French kissing for a few minutes when she pushes me back forcefully, from my chest.

"We can slow down if you want, that's fi–" She stops my whisper with one finger over my mouth and her other hand behind my head. She is looking directly into my eyes but not seeing me — she is looking through me, intently. We are frozen like this for a minute. *What the hell is going on?*

Finally, she relaxes and pulls me back down for more. After a few minutes I decide to go for the bra. I'm struggling with the clasp and it's taking a lot of concentration and I think I got half of it unhinged and there's like two hooks or something and.... PUSH! I'm rolled off onto my side and she is on her knees next to me waving her hands at me and mouthing something. She is freaking out. I can't see her face, so I position myself so I can see her lips. Her face is distorted with fear, but I can read the one word on her lips easily as she points to the upper corner of the room.

"Dad!"

Frantically, we scramble around grabbing our clothes, she puts her shirt on and jumps on the couch, motioning me to get behind it. I grab my stuff and get behind the couch without dressing. I figure trying to dress might be the crucial seconds between getting caught or not. I back in and wedge myself behind the couch and the heat register against the wall, in my socks and tighty whities, with my bunch of clothes in a ball under my arm. *Oh crap! My special sneakers.*

I'm trying to catch my breath and keep control when her dad enters the room. She told me later that the conversation went something like this:

"Hey sweetie, what are you doing up?" Dad says.

"Well, I couldn't sleep, so I came down for water and started watching TV," she replies.

He says, "OK, well, get on up to bed, I'll shut everything off."

For me, the conversation was the typical, confusing nonsense commonly heard by hard-of-hearing people everywhere. "Sherpa, zoing whompa. Do zibba drink, flurpity sleep ... well zoomie grnk...." and so on. I'm freaking out.

She leaves the room and he sits down on the couch and starts scanning through the channels. I can feel his weight through the couch pads. I peek my head out from the side of the couch and see my special sneakers over by the TV. I can see his hand on the armrest of the couch. I'm totally freaking out. We're practically touching, with the couch cushions between us. I can feel his every move. Her dad works hard and likes a bit of Scotch at the end of the week, so he was probably kind of groggy at this time of night on a Friday. *He doesn't notice the sneakers? Or he thinks they're hers? Or her older brother's?* He's changing channels still but finally settles in on some late-night news.

Crap. I'm in bad shape. I'm on my side, jammed in behind the couch, in a fog of dust, in my undies. Dad is watching the news, and I'm allergic to her cat. *What if the cat comes? Crap.*

I'm a fit 16-year-old, but after about an hour of this, my ribs, back, shoulders and hips are cramping up and getting numb. I cried silently for about 20 minutes already, and now I think I might be falling asleep. The news is still on.

The rest of the night was a haze of stinging pains, weeping, silent cursing, praying, dozing on and off, and weird silent images from the TV.

My girlfriend came down around 5:30 a.m. and woke her dad and got him to go upstairs to bed. She dragged me out from behind the couch, and I remember we actually laughed and giggled as I climbed out the window.

Her name is Rio and she dances on the sand. I'm feeling better, and some of the aches and pains are diffusing through the peddling as I ride back up to my house. It's early morning and almost full light, but I don't care at this point. I go right up the driveway and put the bike around the back of the garage and stand up the old ladder that is stationed along the back wall there. Back up and over the garage, across the ledge, back into the window to my room. The note is still there on the bed. The note says, *Mom/Dad, I went out, don't worry, I'll be back. Everything is OK.*

May 16, 2014, 1:53 a.m.

Dear Steve,

At least the cat didn't show up! Your deafness has made you more clever, and it's forcing you to think outside the box. I wonder if the slow decline into silence has forced your creativity in ways you might not have ventured. Your music? Your art? Career? Maybe all areas of your life? Maybe you as a person!? … I wonder. Regardless, you took some chances back then, huh? Nice. You need to keep taking chances, man!

Go for it!
Steve

Many-Job Man

By senior year, some friends started calling me "Many Job Man." My first job was probably doing chores in the house, which my mom and I negotiated into a regular weekly moneymaker. There was also the occasional lemonade stand or vegetable stand we ran off the main road at the end of our street. Then my brother and I started a snow-shoveling business on our block. We would get up early, shovel our driveway and walkway, and try to get to all the elderly neighbors' houses before any other kid-crews would reach our block. After a while, we earned regular customers and they would save the job for us.

When I reached 13, I was old enough to get a "Circulars" route. This is like a newspaper route without tips. You needed to be 14 or 15 for a newspaper route. The Circulars was an advertisement paper. I would pack all these advertisements into individual yellow plastic bags; hang them on my handlebars, bike baskets and other bags that I carried on my body; then Wednesday and Saturday mornings, I would ride around and throw them onto people's porches.

In the same vein as snow shoveling, I developed trust within the neighborhood and started doing odd jobs such as cleaning gutters, doing dump runs, and landscaping. Regulars would call my mom or come by and ask me if I wanted a certain job, or if I could do a certain job. They never called me directly on the phone.

In high school, I started digging clams. I got my own boat, engine and gear and worked as a bayman or "digger." I would wake up early, go down to the harbor, row out to my 16 ft. flat-bottom boat and motor out to the bay. The clamming rake is an iron basket–type rake with long teeth that you drag through the mud. It's connected to a series of aluminum pipes culminating with a T-handle. I would find the right depth, adjust my pipes so that the teeth angle was optimum, tighten everything, and pull on that T-handle for 5 - 6 hours. Dragging those teeth through the mud, digging up clams and dumping them into bushel baskets in my boat every 10 or so minutes. Best. Job. Ever. Still to this very day. Best job ever.

April 16, 2014, 2:22 a.m.

Dear Steve,

You know what I noticed here? All of these jobs have two things in common. One, they were influenced, encouraged and supported by your parents, and two, they all seem to have you working alone, in a quiet setting, without the need to communicate too much. Interesting.

So, shoveling snow. It would be a snow day, right? Your father would probably need to be at work though, and your mother would make you shovel the driveway and walkway. Then that one day, remember? … As you finished, she yelled out the door, "Christopher! Steven! Go see if Mr. Ray wants his driveway shoveled." Your first shoveling job! Encouraged by your mom, working with Chris, in a quiet setting, without much communication.

The Circulars route. Your mom set this up with the company after you asked for a job like Chris's. She said, "Yeah, you're going to need a regular income now that you're getting older." Encouraged by your mom, working alone in a quiet setting, without the need to communicate.

Odd-job handyman. Remember the day you asked for money for the Fireman's Fair? Your mom said, "Go see if Mrs. Szokoli, across the street, needs anything done at her place. Look, there's a lot of leaves and branches down over there." Your first customer as a handyman! Encouraged by your mom, working alone, and not much communication or hearing needed.

Clamdigger. Your dad practically built the boat, fronted you the money for the engine and taught you how to do it all. Encouraged by your dad, working alone, and no communication needed.

I see a lot of support here from your folks. Remember how often your dad would go out clamming with you until you got comfortable out there alone? Every weekend, and he would take off early some days and go with you in the afternoon. Remember when he would go and get your grandfather from the city, and all three of you would go clamming? They would talk in Italian and broken English and you couldn't understand them with the hearing loss and the wind, but it didn't matter. You just liked being out there with them. Remember how your grandpa would just point to where you should dig. "Dig-ah here-ah!" he'd demand. "No! Dig-ah there-ah!" He would direct you in the broken English he used with you. Trying to get you to dig up the *scungilli*, the conch snail that he liked to cook and eat. "Grandpa! C'mon. I need to get clams. Clams are money! Scungilli—no money!" you said. "More-ay scungilli!" he'd say, smirking. "Dig-ah there-ah!" He taught you something there, huh?

Interesting. Maybe you were dealing with and figuring out how to navigate work with your hearing loss even then, without even knowing it. All your friends had jobs as waiters, clerks, or in sales, and you tended to seek out quiet environments in which you worked alone, without the need to hear or talk to people.

Why was digging clams your "best job ever"? You should look a little closer at that. Did you like the isolation? Was it just a relief from trying to "hear" everyone everywhere else? An escape? A retreat maybe? Just you and the bay and the rake. A place to chill and work without the constant strain of trying to hear in society.

Well, Steve, they taught you well, and you listened and learned. You used that knowledge and your ingenuity to figure this stuff out and lay the foundation for your careers as a handyman and an educator. You might benefit to revisit some of those lessons.

Good job,
Steve

Audiologist Report 1990 – 1999, Age 20 – 30

<u>Hearing Status</u>: Moderate to severe hearing loss. Bilateral, sensorineural. Approximately 65 – 75 percent loss.

<u>Hyperacusis</u>: High sensitivity to loud, sharp sounds.

<u>Tinnitus</u>: Tinnitus holding steady as a high-pitched white noise at about 30 percent blanket over the residual hearing.

<u>Notes</u>: The right ear is degrading more quickly than the left and causing some balance and dizziness issues. Not using hearing aids. Learning ASL.

Wait! What?

Like most Deaf and hard-of-hearing people, sometimes I just nod my head to keep friends and family from incessant repetition, exaggerated mouth and lip movements, or long and irritating clarifications. This "nodding in agreement" habit is just a bad idea. Bad for communication, bad for genuine interactions, and it can get you in a lot of trouble. I learned just what a bad idea this is in my sophomore year of college.

Frat Boy

I'm sitting on this old Salvation Army couch next to the windows. This is the shared suite room that joins the three bedrooms. I share this suite with five other guys from around the state whom I met over the last year. The rooms occupy the corner of the third floor of my dorm, which happens to overlook the archway entrance to the whole quad. The usual state school crap is scattered around the room: pizza boxes, trash, trippy Salvador Dali posters, magazines and the general assortment of college nonsense.

Everyone in the room runs over to the windows behind me. I'm confused. I have approximately 65 percent hearing loss at this point and miss a lot. I'm wondering if our friend is locked out again. I go check it out with my suitemates at the windows. It's the frat guys marching and chanting. I like this! I don't know much about fraternities beyond the Animal House movie, but I know rhythm and chanting. There is rhythm and chanting going on in my head 24 hours a day! The pledges — guys who want to get into the frat — are in a line, marching, each with his left hand on the shoulder of the guy in front. They stomp in rhythm, and the big guy in the back or the pledge master leads chants, and the rest of them repeat it. All in rhythm and cadence. I love this! This is the football frat, and it's reminiscent of military drills I see in the movies. These guys are big, big man-guys. They stomp loudly and they chant loudly.

"I love this shit!" I say, rocking my head.

My friends in college had started to call me Stevie Ray, in connection with the famous guitarist Stevie Ray Vaughan and the fact that I played a lot of guitar.

"Stevie Ray! Sherbouti con mezle ... rucker nouble ... urder, ith me?" asks my friend Greg, who lives across the archway.

Uhhhhh…. "Yeah," I reply, with the accompanying agreement nod of the head.

About a week later, I enter my suite room to find Greg and three other guys with purple bandanas on their heads. Greg has another one in his hand, and he is holding it out for me.

Greg says, "Stevie Ray! You ready for this? This is Rex, Bart and Teddy. They are pledging with us too."

Wait! What?

Greg says, "Stevie Raaaaay! You're not backing out on me, are you? You said last week that you were going to pledge with me!" Pledges of this frat must wear this purple bandana for nine weeks, never taking it off.

Uh-oh! Shit! "Yeah, right … let's do this. Nice to meet you guys," I say while shaking hands. I do like to challenge myself and push boundaries a little, but I'm on the edge with this one. It might be a little far-reaching.

Greg is a pretty big guy. These other three guys are big-big guys with big muscles and other bumps on their bodies. Square jaws and crew cuts. Tight shirts. Weight-lifting stretch marks on their biceps. I'm an athletic, averaged-sized, long-haired music guy, and I'm pledging the football frat. Ha ha! This is going to be nuts and a hell of a challenge.

The basis of pledging the fraternity seemed to entail the forced bonding of a small group of guys. It mimicked the structures and activities of basic training in a military unit. A mainstay of the pledging experience was what they called the lineup. A "pledge master" would call a lineup, and the pledges would have to line up, in five minutes, in uniform: work boots, blue jeans, gray sweatshirt and the purple bandana. There were one or two lineups a day. The pledge master would yell at us, tell us we suck, tell us we're losers, then force us to do push-ups and sprints and march and chant. I love this shit. I know their game.

Being the smallest and one of the shortest, I was up toward the front of the line of nine guys. Being in front of people means having people behind you, right behind you, out of eyesight. Not good for a hard-of-hearing guy. It's important to keep your eyes forward at all times in this type of drill, until a pledge master yells "Eyeballs!" Not good for a hard-of-hearing guy trying to decipher the different instructional screams from the pledge master.

Did he just yell 'Eyeballs!' or some other two-syllable word?

Being in front of people means having a bigger guy six inches behind you yelling chants at full volume. Not good for a hard-of-hearing guy with hyperacusis, a sensitivity to loud sounds. Bart was a serious weight lifter with a strong, deep voice. Every time Bart yelled a reply, I'd involuntarily cringe. This went on for about a week until I got him to understand that yelling in my ears felt like a little electrical shock to the nervous system, which the brain interprets as pain.

"When I say left!" yells the pledge master.

The line replies, "The left foot" [*pain, jolt*] "strikes the deck!" [*pain, electrical shock*].

Bart was supportive about figuring out how to solve this problem with me. He started working on dropping the volume of his voice while making it look like he was yelling loudly and even just mouthing the replies without making a sound. It worked. The pledge masters didn't notice or make an issue of it, and I was more at ease without the jolting electric shocks.

But being hard of hearing created other issues with call-and-reply chanting. The pledge master and the big guy in the back led the calls, and the little hippie deaf guy in the front wasn't hearing the call right and was screwing it all up. "Maybe we should give him a haircut and he'll be able to hear better!" screamed the pledge master. "You're a bunch of losers! Maybe we'll shave your heads! Bunch of losers, never going to become brothers!"

We had to do a lot of push-ups the first few days until the pledge master decided to switch things around this pledge session because of "the little guy with the disability." He wanted the little "retarded" guy to lead some of the chants instead. "Can you do that, you scum? Can you losers do that? You want to be brothers? Listen to the retard! Get your shit together!"

Hell yeah! I get to lead some of the chanting! I love this shit. The line was an instant sensation in the quad and frat. We were rocking it. Making up rhythms and chants was just as natural to me as running football plays was for them. After a few weeks, this pledge line was rocking, grooving and harmonizing. We were tight, yet nuanced … like a band. The pledge master asked me to learn some Beatles songs on guitar. I would play them and the rest of the line would sing. We practiced our show of Beatles songs and some of my made-up chants and then performed in front of the various dorm cafeterias around campus and off campus in the fraternity houses. The pledge masters probably thought this was embarrassing and degrading for us, but I was loving it.

It was about this time that the frat gave us our pledge names. They named me Freedom Rock after a popular set of CDs consisting of music from the 1960s. There was a commercial on late-night TV in the late 80s that featured a long-haired hippie-looking guy with a red bandana on his head. Mine was purple, but Freedom Rock stuck, and I had to write it on the back of my gray sweatshirt uniform.

About five weeks into pledging, we're instructed to meet at the frat bar for a lineup. It was packed as usual with all the sports and cheerleader–type students. They line us up in front of everyone, yell at us and make us do a couple shots of tequila. Some push-ups, another shot or two, some more yelling, and we get to break it up. I retreat to the far corner of the venue because some of the brothers are getting really drunk in the corner by the door. Those guys like to fight. I keep to the other end of the bar for as long as I can.

Damn! One of the drunk brothers is climbing up to stand on the bar. He is obviously wasted — red-faced and swaying a bit. He signals the bartender to cut the music. Luckily, I have a direct line of sight to his lips.

"Eyeballs!" he screams.

"Snap!" All the pledges reply in unison.

He is slurring his words. He is a big, scary, sloppy-drunk brother with crazy eyes. Wolf eyes. Drunk, crazy wolf eyes. He's been in fights. Heads smashing into walls with blood squirting kinds of fights. I've seen them. I'm scared of this dude. *What the hell am I doing here?*

"When I say left!" he screams.

"The left foot strikes the deck!" we reply with an accompanying stomp of the left foot on "deck."

Ouch! Shit, it's getting loud.

"When I say right!" he screams.

"We raise our fists and fight!" we reply with an accompanying right-hand fist pump on "fight."

Shit. Fight? No man, no fighting tonight.

"Line up! Out front! Right now!" he demands.

All the pledges head to the door and everyone is moving out of the way, creating pathways for us. It's a bit surreal. We get outside and immediately fall into line at attention. Other brothers and various onlookers are coming out to see what happens. Crazy

Wolf-Eyes staggers out and immediately starts yelling at us, pacing back and forth in front of the line, angry as hell. Spitting, screaming … I can't get a solid line on his lips and I don't know what he's carrying on about, but he's pissed and drunk. He makes us do some push-ups. *OK, I got this, even with the tequila sloshing around in there.* He makes us march in place and do some call-and-reply chanting. *Cool.* We are doing well. He makes me lead one of my chants. *Cool!* We are tight and I am used to performing for crowds. We nail it. Crazy Wolf-Eyes settles down a bit and dismisses the line.

We did a lot of crazy things during the lineups, incorporating both physical and mental training, all in the name of bonding. I realized a lot of it was abusive, but so far I was enjoying the challenge and navigating through the confusion from being hard of hearing.

Hell Week

Finally we arrive at Hell Week, the last week of pledging. This is a weeklong lineup when they yell at us a lot more, make us do a lot more running and push-ups, don't let us shower all week, make us march everywhere together, make us sleep together and live in a 10x10 space in the suite room, make us do weird things with raw eggs, and then lots of really crazy stuff that I will never talk about. I had a ball this week. I found this week of challenges to be one of the defining times in my life.

It's the middle of Hell Week and we are lined up in the suite room. We are tired, sore and stinking. The pledge master is lecturing us about brotherhood and all that baloney. I'm pretty tired because I was on "guard duty" last night, watching the dorm hallway.

I'm not really paying attention, and he is saying, "Dranken von wiggen ponduzco … vort gromba … weeka … blah blah blah," and then points at me. I look at him. "… And I think Stevie Ray should volunteer for this and lead you off, OK?" he asks.

Uhhhhhhhh…. I hesitantly nod in agreement and say, "Sir, yes sir." *Crap, I did it again. I've got to stop doing this. Volunteer for what?*

"OK great, who else? We need five of you pledges for this. Pick your champions," he says. *Champions? Crap!* Four more of my pledge brothers volunteer, and I'm starting to panic. I'm looking at Greg and he's smiling and nodding and getting all psyched up. He volunteered.

The pledge master keeps cracking the door to check the hallway, asking another brother if he is ready yet. I don't get a chance to ask Greg what we're doing before a couple other brothers come in with two big black Hefty bags of stuff.

"OK, let's get the champions warmed up a little bit! You guys psyched? Who's first?" asks a brother, and everyone points to me. He pulls out a funnel and some six-packs of Molson Golden beer. *Crap! Man, really?*

"How many beers for Stevie Ray?" he asks my pledge master. They settle on four. *Whew! Doable ... I think?*

"Ste-vie Ray! Ste-vie Ray! Ste-vie Ray!" They are all chanting.

The beers go down quicker than I would have imagined, and I don't throw up. Another guy did six and threw up. Another guy did seven and didn't throw up.

"Sir, can you review the rules for the match?" I ask the pledge master while someone is puking in the big garbage pail. Greg is standing with me.

"The rules for the match? Stevie Ray, there is only one rule when you go out there. No 'Full Frontal.' Keep your panties on," he says.

Wait! What?

Greg is looking at me and nodding excitedly. "Steve, man! You're gonna rock this! Read my lips. All the girls from the quad are in the common area down there. They are going to introduce you and then play that frat song they've been playing. You need to do a strip show down the steps and into the common area and do some poses. Then they do the same for the rest of us. Keep your undies on, or we'll get in trouble. You're gonna rock!"

Poses? Undies? I really need to make the switch to boxers.

The music is cranking and they push me out the door. There are about 50 girls surrounding the steps on the balcony and in the lower commons. By the time I get around the balcony and to the top of the stairway, my work boots and shirt are off and I'm gyrating my privates into the railing like it's a stripper's pole. I'm totally into it. Something happened with the music and the crowd, and I went into performance mode. I was having a great time. Everyone was yelling. By the time I got to the lower commons, I didn't even care that I was in my nasty tighty whities. But I know I definitely would not have volunteered for this one if I'd heard the lead-in.

A Lover or a Fighter?

Finally, it's the last day of Hell Week, and there is one final lineup and activity before they let us go shower, change and meet up for the induction ceremony. It's some sort of tradition they do every year. It's been six nights now, and the line is a mess of blood, sweat and tears ... and eggs. We line up and march downstairs to the basement common room. All the brothers are there, yelling and cheering. They let us break out of line for some reason, and it's a big mass of confusion for me. Yelling, cheering and patting on shoulders. Pushing and playful shoving.

The pledge master is walking around with a top hat held upside down in his hands. He is yelling inspirational-type stuff and instructions for the pledges among rounds of cheers from the fraternity. He's getting the pledges pumped up for something. They do not look happy about finishing this whole thing tonight. *Now what?* I don't know what's going on. *Come on, man! What now?* After a few minutes of this, he comes over to me and puts one hand on my shoulder and quiets everyone down.

"Tonight, we start things off with Freedom Rock!" he yells, and everyone cheers. "And the headliner tonight, to end this nine weeks, in accordance with fraternity traditions, will be Brontosaurus versus Bo Mo Fo." The brothers are yelling and screaming, going wild. Bront is our end-of-the-line guy. He's our biggest pledge. Bo Mo Fo is a frat alumna and he's about 27 years old. His younger brother, Donnie, is in school and is the vice president of the frat. Bo is the biggest brother in the frat. He is maybe the biggest person in the state. He is Bo Mo Fo. He is the size of Shrek. He hot-iron-branded the frat letters across the width of his entire 24-inch chest. I am not sure if he has a job right now or takes classes. He is just Bo Mo Fo. He is a monster, and he's my good friend. He sometimes sleeps on the couch in my suite.

I find Brontosaurus in the crowd, and he looks pale and defeated, like a limp bunny rabbit in the jaws of a mountain lion.

Brontosaurus versus Bo Mo Fo? Versus? Oh, man. Are we sumo wrestling? I'm hoping for a Nintendo showdown.

As I have my hand in the top hat, mixing the folded papers around, trying to magically draw Big Mitch, Donnie comes through the crowd with two pairs of boxing gloves.

Wait! What? Oh crap!

Big Mitch, although well-proportioned and muscular, is one of the smallest guys in the frat. I didn't pick Big Mitch. I picked Tiny! Tiny fucking Tim! The guy that has been harassing and threatening Brontosaurus all semester about Bront liking Tiny's sister. He's got those wolf-type eyes too, he never smiles, and he's not tiny like the name suggests. He's like a running back, bodybuilder guy.

We are lacing up the gloves, and I'm just terrified. Terrified to take a shot to the head and mess up my ears more. *This is stupid.*

I plead, "Tiny, sir, I can't get hit in the head, my ears, you know? It might damage me, mess me up forever, you know?" He looks me in the eyes and smiles. *He smiled! What a bunch of psychos!*

I've never hit anyone before. *I'm going to punch him in the arm and fall down. Curl up. Fuck this. I don't give a shit anymore.* Everyone's yelling. I pump up a little and punch Tiny Tim in the stomach. No reaction. Cheers. I do it again. He smiles. I double-jab him in the shoulder and chest and wind up for a big right to … I have no idea where. It lands on his other shoulder, and he pulls back and unloads. I put my arms up, turn to the side, and his fist connects with my tricep/shoulder. I fall back about 6 feet into the crowd and go down. *Holy shit!* I'm OK. I start pulling off the gloves and cheering maniacally, raising my arms in the air. I'm trying to confuse them into thinking the match is over. I get the gloves off and high-five with Tiny. Whew, it's over.

Each pledge has a boxing match after me. Some go well, others don't. Bo Mo Fo didn't let Bront take the first punch. He just stared him down, approached, and dropped him fast and hard with one gigantic blow.

We had the inductions that night, and it really felt like an accomplishment. Weird in a way, but the nine of us truly did bond over the few months. We became very close and looked out for each other through the years at the university. And I loved the discipline and the problem-solving scenarios I encountered through the pledging experience. However, I quickly realized I was too much of an independent thinker to continue to participate in the fraternity after inductions, beyond having my band play at some of their yard parties.

All in all, successfully overcoming the pledging challenge is something I often look back on for inspiration. But the nodding in agreement to stuff I don't really understand is a bad habit I still can't totally seem to kick.

June 25, 2014, 12:10 a.m.

Dear Steve,

Fun times, Bro, fun times indeed.

You should remember overcoming those challenges of yesteryear when you're faced with the new challenges of today. You got through it. You worked it out. You had fun!

Proud of you, man. Snap!

With a "Bro Hug,"
Steve

Now What?

I was approaching my third year as an undergrad without a declared major. I needed to decide on a focus of study. I was really focusing on music, submerging myself into every music scene available and doing a lot of music writing, performing and recording. A lot of jamming and traveling to different colleges to jam with Mark and my music buddies. But I needed to pick a major and think about how I could make money while playing music. This was the first time I really had to take into account my hearing loss, its progression and its limitations in regard to my nonmusical plans for the future. I had considered teaching and thought I could do that and play music. But how was I going to teach as a hearing-impaired, or more likely, a Deaf person? I thought maybe I should look into a career with fewer face-to-face communications, such as computer coding. Something where there aren't a few hundred questions a day asked by confused youths who mumble a lot, talk softly, talk into their hands, have hair covering their faces and generally are still learning communication skills. Do I want to be in situations like that every day?

I ran it around and around and realized that a good path would be to teach Deaf and hard of hearing kids. My hearing loss was moderate to severe at this point ... I might go deaf ... I should work with kids like me! I signed up for the Education Program and later focused on Special Education, Severe Needs and Hearing. I started sign language classes, and things kept rolling in that direction.

May 1, 2014, 1:17 a.m.

Dear Steve,

I know what you're thinking. You're feeling a little repressed from the hearing loss. You're feeling controlled, like some of your free will has been taken away. You think the deafness put a limit on what you could do?

There are two sides to this, Steve. The deafness helped give you direction but also limited your range. You got dealt a bad card, you were given a heavy cross to bear, you got a flaming bag of dog poop on the front porch. However you want to look at it, it is what it is, and it's how you react to it that counts. Hey man, remember, you aren't the only one. Everyone has their roadblocks to overcome, and you did a good job with yours. You are pretty lucky overall, and you did well with this. Good choice going into education. I'm proud of you—you're helping kids, man! You took what you had and you worked it, and it worked out pretty well. Sure, the deafness closed some doors, but look at what it opened up for you. You have a great job, you're in a continuous learning environment, and you're making the community better! Way to go, man!

With a butt slap and pat on the back,
Steve

Legally Deaf

When I was around the age of 20, the doctors starting labeling me as "deaf." I'd go into the office after the assessment in the booth and they would look at my charts and say something like, "How long have you been deaf?" I'm thinking … *Doctor Dude, I'm not really deaf, am I? I mean, I can still hear that drum beat from the same song I've been listening to for five years. And that bass line? You mean like "functionally deaf" or some derivation of "deaf," right?* I didn't identify as Deaf for a long time.

At a certain decibel (dB) loss, they start to label you legally deaf. A hard thing to swallow, but this legally deaf label probably got me out of at least three traffic violation tickets over the years. I get to put "Driver is deaf" on my license and can tell cops, "I am Deaf but read lips kind of well in certain optimal situations." It makes them feel a little bad, and they give you a break sometimes. One time I even got the policeman to shine the flashlight into his own face so I could read his lips. In my circle, we call that "playing the Deaf card."

Playing the card can have mixed results. For example, my buddy Mark would say at a theater show, "Dude, these seats suck. Play the Deaf card — maybe they'll give us closer seats!" but then they'd move us back into the wheelchair section behind the soundboard workers for "better sound," not up front. Another attempt, in a hotel room: "The captions don't work on this TV. I'm going to play the Deaf card; maybe they'll upgrade me to their Hollywood hotel suite." They moved me into another room with working captions, but it was an old, smelly, smoking room.

But then there was the one day I really felt like I nailed it. I won something, man! Today I hit the jackpot! This is it! Finally! The National Parks Service gave me a lifetime pass to get into all national parks for free! Take that, you hearing bastards! The

Deafies, disabled and seniors are gonna be rocking these parks across the whole nation! Here we come!

Someone at the park entrance booth saw me struggling with understanding the interpreter friend I had with me in the car and handed me the card. That's where the "Deaf card" term came into play for me. And what a day it was! I felt great. Finally, a real, honest break with this. I still can't understand the rangers when they do their programs and tours, but sometimes they supply a written copy of the tour or program.

July 22, 2014, 4:32 a.m.

Dear Steve,

Yeah man, yeah! See? It's good to get out of the basement. Seriously, Steve, get out of the damn basement right now. Stop reading this and go upstairs. Go outside! Take a couple deep breaths and then go do something. The odds of something good happening when you leave the basement are so much higher compared to staying in the basement. Yeah, unexpected bad things might happen out there, and even though you're struggling right now with the deafness, I know you can handle whatever happens. But, dude, remember to stay positive! Sometimes unexpected great things happen out there. You win the game, you hit the jackpot, you meet the person who makes you a fabulous offer, you run into an old friend. If you'd stayed in, you never would've met your beautiful, loving wife and soulmate. It's only because you were out there. Good things won't magically appear in your unfinished, moldy-smelling, needs-a-paint-job basement, man! Get out there.

Knuckle tap,

Love,
Steve

The Swivel-Roller-Chair

Professor Martin's classroom is decorated with posters of teachers reading books with young students with disabilities, and students with disabilities presenting projects or acting in skits or plays. She is very aware of and knowledgeable about people with disabilities and their rights. She's teaching the graduate level class, Special Education: EDU502, Collaboration and Communication. Excellent! She's really going to understand that I'm in flux right now with my communication methods. I'm in between hearing and deaf, in between audio reception and visual reception. Many hard-of-hearing people and late-deafened people commonly feel like they are in between the Deaf culture and the hearing culture, but not really part of either. Oftentimes, they feel as though they are in between languages or communication types as well.

It was a very tough time, with these classes being masters-level with high-end concepts, vocabulary and theories that were new to me. I couldn't understand the level of concepts through the interpreter with sign language yet because I was still learning and mastering the language. Nor could I lip-read the teacher or the conversations around the room because my hearing had declined to a level that made it just impossible to get the cue sounds that lip-readers need. I was "in between" for most of my time in higher education.

Professor Martin's class was always set up in a circle of desks so that we could all see each other. There were about 25 students, and she would sit in the circle, but she would also be outside the circle, writing on the board or working the overhead projector. At this time in my education, I was using an FM system supported by copies of the lecture notes that I would borrow from one of my many friendly classmates, because this method seemed to gain me the most comprehension of the material. An FM system is a mic that hooks onto the speaker's shirt, and the user wears headphones, in my case, or connects it directly to a hearing aid. This worked great for me if I could see the speaker's lips. I could get above 90 percent comprehension with this method when looking directly at the speaker.

Fortunately, Professor Martin did not lecture us to death and supported class conversation, thus the circle setup. However, unfortunately, the circle setup is a bad situation for a Deaf guy with the FM system. For the first class or two, I just suffered through the 45 minutes of class conversations, not knowing what the heck was going on. *This sucks.* The isolation. The feeling of confusion first, then frustration, then anger, then trying to think of a solution, then frustration again, then boredom, and finally acceptance that I'm screwed on this one. I'm trying to turn invisible, but eventually, the teacher will look for me, then point at me and say something like, "What do you think? What would you do with that type of student?"

Oh crap.

Sometimes I would just say, "I don't know. I just don't know what I think right now." Sometimes, if I got a smidgen of the information and was feeling cocky, I would try to bullshit through it with some half-assed baloney and a few jokes. "Uh ... with that student I would call his mom, definitely call home and maybe slap the back of the student's hand with the ruler!" Sometimes I played the reversal game of answering the question with another question: "Well, I was wondering what you, as an experienced teacher, did about that back when you were teaching high school."

This one time, in Professor Martin's class, I had a revelation, or a breakdown, or maybe just a breakthrough finally, and I let it rip. "What do I think? I'm thinking about how screwed I am. I'm not understanding diddly-squat right now. I have no idea what you-all are talking about. Holy shit! I mean, what am I doing here like this? I've been sitting here for 30 minutes looking at your faces and making up imaginary conversations between you. Making up stories about you. Little fantasies and dramas and comedies. Oh man, I'm going to be teaching a roomful of kids and I am paying for this, and I am sitting here in fantasyland and realizing that this sucks. I need to figure something out! What am I going to do? I really do want to know what you're talking about. I'm kind of tired of sitting out all the time, and for so long. Can I move into the middle of the circle with that swivel-roller-chair?"

Thus began a two-year stretch of the swivel-roller-chair until I got better at ASL and finally enlisted a full-time interpreter. I would cruise inside, back and forth on the spokes of the circle, trying to lip-read each person as the class conversed. Whooosh! Zoooom, across the circle. It was nuts. The teachers supported it, and the students were patient and eventually asked to pass the FM mic around during discussions.

February 27, 2014, 3:06 a.m.

Dear Steve,

Dude. On the one hand, that's just pretty crazy. Swiveling around in a masters-level class at a university like that. Funny, man. On the other hand, hell yeah! You had a specific problem and you figured a way through it. You had to think outside the box! You've been doing it your whole life. What are you dealing with now, Steve? Work it, work around it. You can do it, man. Remember when you were going to leave the Education Program because of the hearing loss? You didn't quit; you went ahead and switched over to Deaf Education and learned sign language. Remember when you started your handyman business and you were scared to go to hearing people's houses? You didn't quit, you worked on approaches and appropriate communication devices to help you work with hearing people. It all worked out, remember? Remember when you couldn't perform with the band anymore because the proximity to the drums was blocking out every other sound? Remember what you did instead of quitting music performance? You made the plexiglass folding wall to put up between your guitar rig and the drums. It worked, Steve! You have to keep trying until you find a solution that works. Then build on it and modify it. If it fails again, you will find another solution. It is all available to you, if you open up and let it in and are willing to try.

Go forth and prosper,
Steve

Phone Allies

I'm pretty sure the last time I put a phone to my ear to try to have an actual conversation was in February, 1997. For the decade leading to that last call, phone use was becoming very uncomfortable.

<u>1987 — TV room in my parent's house.</u>

I'm hanging out after my day job, in the back of our house having lunch and watching MTV. Work this summer consisted of digging clams in the morning and working with Gary the postman in the evening. Gary delivered the mail in our neighborhood and ran a landscaping business in the evenings, pretty much on the same route.

My mom pops her head into the room and swings the old long coiled phone line across her head as she switches the headset to the other side so I can read her lips.

"Steven, I have the Deaf kid on the phone, we are setting up a time for tutoring." She says.

"Huh? You're talking to a Deaf guy right now?

"Steven, the tutoring. The sign language tutor. He's a kid, a young man, like you. We talked about this. Wednesday at 2:00? OK?" she says.

"How are you talking to them on the phone?"

"Steven! I'm not talking to him directly, I'm talking to an operator person. Steve! Wednesday at 2:00?" she asks again.

"You are talking to an operator? Then they call the Deaf guy?"

"Steven! We are all talking right now!" she yells.

"So this Deaf guy can speak?"

"Steven! He types, the operator speaks to me, there's typing and talking … Operator please tell Abe that Steven will be there at 2:00 on Wednesday. OK, thanks, please tell Abe goodbye." She goes all the way across the house to the kitchen to hang up the phone and comes back. "It's some kind of new thing. Deaf people can call not-Deaf people through this special operator that types. Wednesday at 2. Here's the address."

My mom pushed to set up some sign language tutoring that summer when she realized I wasn't using or benefiting from hearing aids. I went once a week or so and became friends with Abe. I started getting into sign language and conceptual imagery that summer and started to see how the ASL language system allows for flexibility around individual creativity in expression. That artistic, creative aspect was a big draw for me.

Later that summer, when I had some vocabulary under my belt, Abe told me about that first conversation he had with my mom. The operator needs to type everything they hear, along with explanation points. Like, "Steven! We are talking right now! (Woman is now yelling at her son)." So we had a few laughs because the operator typed the whole conversation between my mom and me for him. He said my mom was cool and doing a very good and important thing for me. I agreed. He said I was going to be a good signer.

1989 — College dorm.

I'm sitting in my suite room with my suitemate Harley, whom I met a year ago, and we're debating the merits, demerits, techniques, and pros and cons of the "prog rock" genre vs. "jam band" genre, using Rush and the Grateful Dead as a basis for our discussion points.

I'm lounging with my guitar on the old Salvation Army couch by the windows, which at this point in the year smells permanently like hot wing sauce and stale beer from the Old Milwaukee beer balls we tapped weekly. Harley is sitting on the Old Salvation Army sometimes-reclining-recliner. Our friend Beverly from down the hall enters without knocking and quietly takes a seat in the other corner near Harley. Beverly wears a permanent smile.

Harley and I are conversing, debating, almost arguing. Beverly is grinning. The phone rings. It's closest to me. They both look at it. I missed the first ring, but as the room goes silent, I understand on the second ring. Harley looks at me with eyebrows raised and I look back with a scrounged up face and shrug my shoulders and take a breath.

I pick it up and put it to my better, left ear, instinctively. "Hello?"

"Hi. Shufta cin Day effa Shnuble? This is forgdum effys," the voice says really fast.

"Hi, yeah, this is Steve. Who's this?"

"FORGUDMN WHYFYS. Shuffa kejdma? Hufta Day shaka-laka!" says the voice. I am sensing agitation, but I give it one more try.

"Sorry, can't hear ya. This is Steve. Who are you asking for?"

"I am ASKING for day vah! KNOTTEN FORSHEKTO KRAPPEN SHLOCK! FORNATO KUMBLE!"

Whoa. I bring the phone over to Harley.

"It's definitely a guy." I say with the handoff.

Harley takes it. "Hi, this is Harley."

The guy is talking on the other end.

"Dude, the guy is hearing-impaired," Harley says in his matter-of-fact manner.

Pause.

"No man, the guy can't hear well! What's your deal? He is hearing-impaired."

Another pause and now I can see Harley is turning up the heat in his facial expression and volume.

"Dude! Man! STEVE CAN'T HEAR WELL! HE'S HARD OF HEARING! He's got a HEARING PROBLEM! What's YOUR problem?"

Pause.

"Yes! That's Dave's roommate! Dude. Chill. I'll get him!"

Harley gets up slowly and bangs forcefully with the soft side of his fist on my roommate Dave's door, three times, then a pause and breath, and adds a fourth, final, "let-it-all-out-fucking-A" pound. Dave comes out smiling with headphones on and Harley hands him the phone. I look at Beverly. She is smiling and I smile back. It felt pretty good to have an ally.

1995 — Cathy's House.

"OK, let's call 'Sh-Sh-Shh-Chavaaaaaaaaun' now!" Chavaun is a rich ritzy-glitzy 30-something divorced single mom who wants me to move into her garage apartment and become the multi-tasking handyman-do-whatever-needs-doing, glorified houseboy. We usually recite each of my client funny name jingles before we put on serious voices and call them. We just called "Mr. Stanford!" which we scream in military fashion with a salute. He was in the air force. Before that we called "Mrs. Meyers," which we do in a very loving grandmotherly voice because she was my first client in this new business, and she is awesome. Mrs. Meyers thinks I was sent to her by her recently deceased husband, who went deaf from an illness a few years before passing.

"Hi Chavaun! It's Cathy calling back for Steve."

"I'm great, how are you and the kids?"

"OK, I'll ask him."

She covers the mouthpiece with her hand.

Cathy looks to me, smiling. In a soft chuckling voice, she tells me, "She needs you 2 - 4 hours on Friday morning this week, to uhhhmmm ... wrap Christmas presents while her kids are at school!"

"Um ... OK. Hell yeah! Sure. Tell her I'm a great wrapper! It's my specialty." I'm psyched, thinking about getting paid $25 an hour for wrapping presents.

Cathy returns the phone to her head. "Steve says he'll be there at 9. He says wrapping is his specialty. A master wrapper — perfect at corners." They are both laughing.

I have about 20 regular clients, and my friend and next-door neighbor, Cathy, makes all the phone calls for me. I go over to her house each evening and we spend 10 or 15 minutes joking around while she calls and talks to my clients and sets up appointments for me for the week.

January 1997 — Kitchen in my rental house.

My friend Frank goes over to pick up the phone. He is talking and looking at me. I come over and lip-whisper, "Who is it?" Frank talks a bit more, but I can't see his lips. He stops and covers the mouthpiece with his hand, looks directly at me, and says, "It's your brother and he wants to talk to Kim." Kim is a great girl I've been dating for about two years. She is in the living room.

Dread. *Uh-oh.* My mind immediately starts racing to bad thoughts. My dad has been fighting cancer for almost six years at this point and, living in another state, I call once or twice a week to check in but mostly ask yes-and-no questions and try to hear their answers.

I ask Frank to give me the phone and he does.

"Chris, it's Steve. What's going on?" I make extra effort at pronunciation when I talk to my brother because of his hearing loss and my failing speech clarity. He probably does the same. He wears a hearing aid and probably has his on high for phone calls.

"Steve, I have — um ew abao Dad. I called -is doctor and finkel shronto dalking. Can you uner stan? Put Kim on." He says slowly.

"What? Can you say that again?"

"Put Kim on," he says.

"Tell me."

"Put Kim on, I wan to make ur oo uner stan," Chris repeats.

I'm crying now. So is Kim. And Frank.

Kim takes the phone. "Hi Chris, it's Kim."

They talk for a minute and she stops to tell me my dad is OK right now and at home and comfortable. Kim is crying and I'm a mess. They talk a bit more and she hangs up. She explains to me that Chris was able to get the information and prognosis directly from our Dad's doctors. He called to let me know that the doctors all confirm that there isn't anything more they can do and he has a few more months to live.

I can't stop crying, and between sobs I ask Kim to walk with me up to Mark's house, a couple of blocks away. We get there and I still can't breathe enough to talk. Kim explains what's going on and we all spend some time together walking around in circles in Mark's living room.

February 1997 — Kitchen in my rental house.

"OK, Mom, can you put Dad on?" I had just talked to my mom for a minute or two about how things were going. They never told us the prognosis, and if my brother hadn't called the doctors, I am not sure if I would have known. I guess my dad didn't want to burden us. Shortly after this phone call, I decided to take off the rest of the semester of graduate school and spend it at home with my parents.

"Hi Dad. How's it going?"

"Oh, I'm all right." His classic response, never transferring his stuff onto anyone. "How are you? Kim?" he says. He knows I can't hear him well and keeps it all short, loud and clear. I have the phone jammed hard against my left ear.

I'm trying to not start crying.

"We are all good. Listen Dad, I just wanted to tell you that I love you."

Pause.

"Thanks Steve, thanks a lot. I love you too, very much."

This is the only time I told my father I loved him. It is the only time I remember him telling me. We just didn't speak openly about emotions in our family. There was no doubt that we loved each other, and I never needed to hear it from him. Every single day, he showed me through his actions how much he cared and loved me. That's the way he raised me. Never a doubt.

May 19, 2014, 3:11 a.m.

Dear Steve,

I'm proud of you for having the courage to call and say the words to your dad from the heart, knowing that you might not be able to hear his reply. I'm proud that you consistently offered your support to your dad and family throughout his illness.

I'm also proud of you for opening up. I'm proud of you for accepting help from others. I know it's not an easy thing for you to do. Don't forget, like the support you got from your mom, dad and brother, you have a lot of friends and family that care about you and want to help you through the stages of hearing loss. You have many allies and a lot of patient and understanding friends. So many supportive people in your life that are helping you communicate, making phone calls, learning sign language, and writing things down for you.

Remember your allies and people that care about you and support you, Steve. Be open and accepting.

With gratitude,
Steve

ASL Club

I definitely got a few dates back in college with the new label "Legally Deaf." The doctors were right after all! ("He'll be all right. He's good-looking!") In college when I was studying Deaf Education and found I had a knack for American Sign Language, I was asked to run the ASL Tutor Club a few days a week after classes. Oh, yeah! Anybody in the field of Deaf Education, ASL or Deaf Studies knows that the ratio of women to men in these classes is approximately 50 to … 1! Stevie Ray! One girl actually came clean at the tutor room when I asked, "What are you doing here? What do you want to get out of this?" She said, "I heard there was a cute Deaf guy tutoring ASL, and I wanted to check you out." I kept my post at the tutor center through the remaining years at school.

My connection to ASL and Deaf culture grew and often provided the life raft to get through some tough times as well as an avenue to some great times. I can't underestimate the role that ASL played in providing me with a sense of being when all else was failing. A catalyst to self-discoveries, it helped me accept myself and grow to establish my self-identity. Having a communication system and connection to fellow signers and a wonderful culture was a saving grace.

August 16, 2014, 3:45 a.m.

Dear Steve,

Stevie Raaaaay! Dude, see? That door appeared because of your deafness, and you opened it by getting out there, accepting things and trying new things. If you weren't going deaf, you wouldn't have learned ASL or have been asked to run the Tutoring Club, etc., etc.... and hey, man, didn't you meet your beautiful, loving wife and soulmate at that school?

Hugs and kisses,
Steve

You Got Lucky

"I like your music group!" she yelled.

Soup? How'd she know?

"I love soup too!" I burst out. "How'd you know? Did you hear me talking to Nate in class about the green chilies I've been getting at the farmers market? I've been making green chili, my grandma's *pasta e fagioli* and a few different sausage soups. One with beans, a sausage soup with potatoes, and a spicy chilies and sausage soup I'm calling 'Death by Sausage.' I've also been making some really basic brothy soups with spinach and cannellini beans. Do you cook? What kind of soup do you make?"

Whoa buddy. Take it easy. Diarrhea of the mouth there.

I'm driving up the interstate in my old cargo van that I alternately use for doing odd handyman jobs — also carting all the music equipment around for the gigs we've been playing — and for driving back and forth to the nearby university where I'm taking classes, which is about 45 minutes away from the smaller town that I live in. The AC is not working and the windows are all the way down. I'm trying to read her lips through the rearview mirror that I adjust so I can see her face in the front passenger seat. Before this, she hadn't said a word in 10 minutes since the initial "Hello, how are you?" when I picked her up. She has just been silently looking at her books and then writing stuff down.

Is she doing homework? Ugh! Looks like a journal or something of that sort, but she seems very nice.

I'm pretty comfortable with silence, but this is our first carpool up to the university. I think her name is Tracy or Stacy. I'm not good with names because I'm usually distracted from lip-reading by that involuntary glance at the person's hand, for the handshake, which always happens the same instant the person's name is stated during introductions.

So, 10 minutes of silent journaling, then a soup-liking proclamation … cool!

"Um, I have been cooking a bunch lately," she says, and smiles at me in the mirror. "I've been making some Eastern European–inspired soups like borscht. So, beets and cabbage and that kind of stuff."

"Awesome!" I yell.

Did she say cabbage soup? Uh-oh. Pass the salt, please. Well, she cooks, and she likes soup. Stacy or Tracy who cooks and likes soup.

Silence. Wind.

Awkward silence. Wind.

Just driving in my van. On the road. With a hot girl. Journaling, cabbage-soup-eating hot girl.

Silence.

"Do you like the Grateful Dead? Everyone in town seems to, these days," she says through the rearview mirror.

"That new place downtown? I luuuuuuv the Daily Bread!"

Man! This girl is asking all the right questions! But, what the heck was that? You've never, ever done the extended "luuuuuuv" thing, you dork.

"What kind of bread do you like?" I ask her.

"Um, I like really crusty, hearty bread, for dipping into soup. Those kinds of crusty breads," she yells over the wind and engine noise from the highway.

Yes! Indeed! Yes ma'am! Wowsers.

Calm and cool. "Me too, totally. Nothing like a good crusty crust." *Nothing like a good crusty crust? Dork!*

Silence. Wind.

Driving in my vaaaaaan.

With a soup-eating ma'am.

On the road in my vaaaaaaan.

She's a crust-dipping hot girl.

That last part doesn't rhyme, man. Try, "She's a crust-dipping fan."

Awkward silence. Wind.

So, I'm thinking I better check in about the windows. "Are you comfortable in the van? I'm sorry about the AC. We could roll up the windows? Sorry about the smell too. I've had this van since high school and I use it a lot for work, doing odd jobs and construction stuff. Sorry about the gasoline smell, and the dirt. Do you want to roll up the windows? You can roll up yours and I'll keep mine open. Do you want to roll them up halfway?" The wind is blowing her hair all around, and she's smiling, shaking her head "no" and giving me a thumbs-up.

She likes the van! And maybe, just maybe, the man in the van! The van man!

Silence.

She waits until I glance at her in the rearview mirror and then says, "So, you play guitar."

"Yeah, I saw your car! Remember? When we met after classes last week to set up carpools with Nate. It's cool. I like it. Old cars are cool! Is it an oldie but a goodie? Do you have to do a lot of work on it? Seems like every few months, I need to get something done on the van."

An oldie but a goodie? Dude! You're dorking out!

She smiles. "Um, yeah. I need to put work into it way too often. Just two months ago I needed to put in a new radiator. It's the last of the 'thousand dollar cars' that I'm ever getting. I just can't afford anything over a grand, you know?" *Huh, what was that? I'm not following.* "I really love this car, but would you believe this is the third 'thousand dollar car' I've had since high school? But I still love it!" she exclaims. *Huh? I missed it. Did she change the subject? She changed the subject back to food, man! Is she talking about candy now? She keeps doing air quotes around Hundred Thousand Dollar Bar. That's a really good one! With the caramel and the krispies. Is it possible that this girl is more into food than I am? Wowsers!*

Better play it safe and not say anything.

"Yeah, cool. Totally," I say and nod my head repeatedly.

Maybe I should put on some of my band's songs. See if she is into music. Let her know that I'm a musician. The guitar-playing man with the van!

We drove back and forth twice a week that semester and became good friends. Next semester she invited me and my on-again, off-again girlfriend over to her boyfriend's place for "game night." A couple weeks later, they showed up at one of my gigs. A couple months later, we were both single. A couple weeks after that, we started the semester carpool, but our classes weren't aligned, so we didn't drive together. A couple weeks later, I started to put Hundred Thousand Dollar Bars on her windshield early in the morning on the days she was driving to classes without me. A couple weeks after that, she invited me to go skiing. A couple weeks later, we met up at a party. A couple weeks later, I was throwing pebbles up at her window at midnight asking to hang out, unsuccessfully. A couple weeks after that, I planned my make-it-or-break-it move for that Friday night. Although kinda cheesy, I was going to do the window pebble-toss with a guitar serenade. Turns out I didn't need to. Tracey invited me over on Thursday.

May 6, 2014, 2:15 a.m.

Dear Steve,

Stevie Raaaaaaay! You know it's right when you know it's right! Right? Some things you just know! You know? The deafness didn't really have anything to do with you guys getting together, right? It would've happened or it wouldn't have, regardless of your deafness, right? Tracey saw the whole person, beyond the deafness. I know the deafness plays a major part in your life and identity, but remember, it is not that big a deal to most people. It's not your main identity, it's a part of the whole. Tracey never even mentioned it those first few years. She didn't make it a factor in your relationship. Made you feel good, right? She just learned some sign language, repeated things, wrote stuff down and just took it all on as it came. Remember that, Steve—"Take it all on as it comes." Man, you got lucky. Jackpot!

Congratulations!
Steve

The Booth

"Say *baseball*," the robot voice says.

"Say *ice cream*."

"Say *cowboy*."

"Say *baseball*."

It's like a 1950s creep show in here. Like an episode of the Twilight Zone. You'd think they could lighten this place up a little. Maybe some sconces on the wall? A plant? Mood lighting? A total creep show with the crazed, bug-eyed monkey guy in the corner, in his glass box, banging on his cymbals when the light flashes. And the drugged-out pink elephant from the land of Oz in her glass box on the other side. Seriously? The dizzying soundproof walls with their trippy patterns and the outer-space beeps and tweets. The audiologist's robotic voice is an alien preparing me for probing. Why does she keep repeating the same two-syllable monotonic words over and over? "Baseball," "Ice cream," "Cowboy" … "Baseball," "Ice cream," "Cowboy".… Fuck you, lady! It's been 10 years since I had this hearing test, and I remember why I stopped having this done. This is terrifying!

The tiny-perimeter but double-thick 4-inch window is like something from an underwater spacecraft. They conference out there with other doctors, but you can't really see them without getting right up against the submarine window. I try to imagine they are talking about how cute and funny I am, but they are probably saying something in the realm of, "He's screwed! That guy is going deaf on the fast train." Then they flick the mic switch and try speaking to me. It's nearly impossible to attain a clear line of vision with the poor lighting and thick, foggy glass window. The voice sounds like a robot on an a.m. radio broadcast. *I can't really hear you! I can't understand the instructions!* If I close my eyes, it seems as though they're standing across the street and way down the block. Nobody here knows ASL? Seriously? Nobody in this whole entire department of hearing sciences knows any sign language? Then the audiologist covers her mouth and wants me to repeat the scary monotonic words again. I'm just going to ride it out and go with saying *ice cream* every time. Or *fuck you*.

Come on! One plant? Maybe a butt massager on the chair? Some water? It's a lot to deal with in there. Especially while knowing that the underlying purpose of the whole visit is to let me know how much more hearing I've lost. I'm not going to get my hearing back. After 30 minutes of this freak show, they open the vacuum-sealed submarine door and the doctors tell me how deaf I am.

February 12, 2014, 2:56 a.m.

Dear Steve,

Dude, wow, you need to relax. Maybe if you relax a little, things might get better or seem better. I know you have a vivid imagination, and the stuffies are definitely weird, but maybe if you relax and work with the doctors a little more, you'll be able to get to a place of better communication with them, which might open more doors to more solutions for you. Maybe you can help change things. You know, "Be the change you want to see"? Maybe put together a presentation for the next state audiologists symposium and try to educate the group about why it's important for audiologists to know some ASL, or other failings of the current environment in the booth. It's your job to raise awareness. If you relax, think on a topic and really focus, you will find a solution.

With love,
Cowboy Steve

Muffs

The sensitivity problem, hyperacusis, got so bad that I started wearing construction-grade Earmuffs or foam Earplugs everywhere. When writing about Earplugs or Earmuffs, I capitalize them because they are that important to me.

Usually I opted for the Earmuffs because I could take them on and off quickly and attempt to communicate. The Plugs were for long-term exposure to loud sounds, such as at a gig or concert, walking around the city or working on a construction job. I would buy the cases of 200 Plugs. I remember being excited when they produced a new type of Earplug that blocked up to 34 decibels — 2 more decibels than the previous model and a lot more comfortable! I've joked that I'm the biggest Earplug consumer west of the Mississippi River.

One of my friends had a girlfriend who laughed really, really loudly. I couldn't comfortably hang out in a social setting with her unless I wore my Earmuffs. Of course, I couldn't hear anyone else talking either. So I would use a pad, paper and pen method, which became a fun after-party-type thing for my group. The next morning we would look over the conversations and the funny things people would write.

I would wear my Earmuffs when doing the dishes. Sometimes, just watching movies with my friends, the volume and explosions would produce sensations of pain inside my head, so I would wear my Muffs. Mowing the lawn, I would wear my Muffs. Any kind of banging or cutting around the house, I'd wear my Plugs. Vacuuming, I'd wear my Muffs. Concerts would be Plugs and sometimes Muffs over them. Going to a bar, I'd wear my Plugs or sometimes my Muffs. I didn't give a shit.

Same results with the paper-and-pen after-party stuff. Even better. Before we went out, my friends would ask me if I had my Plugs or Muffs, because sometimes I'd forget and we'd have to drive back and get some "protection." My friends got so used to it, they started asking about my Muffs when I didn't have them on.

We painted my Muffs and decorated them with sparkles, stickers and flags. I have pairs of Muffs signed by famous musicians I met after a show or backstage in the greenroom. I've had ceremonies when I retired a pair of Muffs. We would stand around the garbage can with candles lit, chanting as I threw them in.

Using hot water and soap, I've washed many an Earplug and lined them up vertically on a towel to air-dry. If you squeeze them out or squeeze-dry with a towel, they deteriorate faster and are not as protective. I have special carry cases for the Earplugs and always have a second pair in my pocket. I also have extra pairs in the cars, guitar cases, backpacks, jackets; double pairs in every toolbox and work-belt; and in the back of friends' and families' utilities drawers or closets in their houses. I do not exaggerate: I might very well be the biggest single consumer of Earplugs west of the Mississippi!

September 1, 2014, 2:54 a.m.

Dear Steve,

Nice, buddy! You did what you needed to do, my man. You protected yourself, you figured out a way to incorporate yourself socially, and you had fun with it. Nice! So what happened recently? Why did you stop having fun? Things changed? Situations changed, right? You got older, you have a family, you lost more hearing, and you're working more. It's just new situations to figure out, man. Just like transitioning from high school to college and figuring out how you were going to manage classes and a social life with the deafness. You figured that out, right? You had fun. Just like transitioning from college to living independently in a new state and figuring out how to start your career with your deafness. You figured that out, right? You had a lot of fun, Steve! Now, I guess, you need to analyze the problems and roadblocks with your new situation and figure out how to manage your family life, career and social life with your deafness. You will, and you'll have fun. You always do.

Rock on, buddy!
Steve

Audiologist Report   **2000 – 2009, Age 30 – 40**

<u>Hearing Status</u>: Severe to profound hearing loss. Bilateral, sensorineural. Approximately 80 percent loss in the left ear and 90 percent loss in the right ear.

<u>Hyperacusis</u>: High sensitivity to loud, sharp sounds.

<u>Tinnitus</u>: Tinnitus holding steady as a high-pitched white noise at about 30 percent blanket over the residual hearing.

<u>Notes</u>: Not using hearing aids because there isn't much to amplify.

Rock and Roll

I formed a bunch of rock-and-roll groups over the years with my buddy Mark. I say "I formed" because no one ever asked me to join their group. Who wants a Deaf guitarist in their group? Back in high school, there was Art Skyd. Later, we formed Sponge. Then we came up with our post-college band, Shankislonvernia, where at one of our first gigs, the owner of the venue promoted us as a touring group from Russia, and we just went along with it for two more years. Then we shortened it to Shankis. There was Wide Mouth Grin, which got a bunch of press from the "Deaf musician" angle. The press and photo shoots were fun, although they didn't get us much exposure outside the local scene. We recorded a lot of music, played a lot of gigs, made some great friends and had a ton of fun.

We're in the middle of the second set at a fairly big ski town gig up in the Rocky Mountains of Colorado. After a fairly successful Rush cover, the crowd is cheering for more, and the drummer is pumped up and pushing us to *start the next damn song*. There's a drunk guy practically spitting in Mark's face, trying to get us to *"play anything by Lynyrd Skynyrd."* There are a few hotties hanging out on Mark's side of the stage, watching his bass magic. I walk over and nervously ask, "Is it doing it now?" because in the brief millisecond of musical space where there are no notes being played in a Rush song, Mark had given me the sign for *something is fucked up with your rig and it's making that buzzing noise again, and I am so sick of this shit*. This is an irritated face with a shaking open hand by the ear, which just so happens to also be the ASL sign for "noise."

Mark has superpowers. How can any normal human play that bass, sing, work the ski town crowd, run the sound system and hear the distinct differences between the different feedback noises coming from my guitar rig?

Mark replies, "Yeah" while signing the "noise" sign.

I lip-read him saying, "Distortion pedal" while he signs "plug in and out"—meaning I should check the power supply cord on the distortion pedal.

He says "Dude" while signing "drunken idiot" and then "Bird-fly-away"—meaning there's another drunken idiot requesting Lynyrd Skynyrd.

He says "Dude" while miming "rope, pull tight"—meaning we should put the rope fence back up to keep the drunk guys from getting too close and stepping all over the equipment.

He says "Dude" while making the "get your shit together" face.

I go back and check the distortion pedal power cord. I look toward Mark and he signs "thumbs up" and nods, signifying that was the problem. Then he signs "tune-up" and "Smitty & Bison" for the next couple of songs, a duo of our originals.

Mark doesn't know ASL. We communicate with sign and body language and facial expressions that just developed and evolved on their own over all the years we've known each other. We've been playing together since sixth grade, over 25 years. We barely need to speak or sign anymore. We can communicate through a whole gig with the music and occasional facial expressions. He has superpowers.

March 18, 2014, 3:06 a.m.

Dear Steve,

I have a couple things to say here, Steve. OK, listen up. Dude-man! Who the hell would play music with you for 25 years? All your going-deaf bullshit, the buzzing noises and feedback you don't hear, the plexiglass dividers all over the room and all your baloney with making sure you got the earplugs and earmuffs. Nobody wants to play music in that situation. Having to do all the phone calls and talking to all the booking agents because you can't talk on the phone. Talking to all the drunk idiots at the gigs after the shows because you can't hear them. Talking to the venue staff because you can't hear them. Talking to the crowd about your deafness and all that promotion bullshit. Talking to the bartenders and ordering your beers because you can't hear them. Taking care of your guitar rig before, during and after each rehearsal and gig. Doing the sound system. Going shopping with you to buy the right-sounding equipment. Recognize your supports, Steve! Buy the guy a beer!

Now I must say, man, you did overcome a big load of crap to figure out how to express yourself with music. Props, man. Seriously. You heard the quiet *hey* voice, and you acted on it. You worked out all the issues, with a lot of help from your supports. And you overcame the deafness to write and perform music. I'm proud of you, man. You let go of your old stories. The ones that started with "Uh, dude, you got a major hearing disability that kinda contradicts your whole plan. I mean ... deaf and music, those two things are kind of contradictory, you know?" Or the one that started with "But I need to work; my job is taking up a lot of time right now…." or the infamous, "I can't do something like that; I will suck at that…."

Thanks for doing stuff, man. Really, please keep doing it. You don't want to be 50 years old and saying to yourself, "I should've finished that record." Or 60 years old and lamenting, "I should've gone on that monthlong backpacking trip through Europe," or 70 years old and saying, "I should've started that woodshop business I always wanted to try, and now it's too late." It's not too late. You can do it. It might take some time; in fact, it probably will. Look in the mirror and have a heart-to-heart with the man in the glass. Ask the man in the glass to help you make a plan, and get support when you need it.

Rock on, Stevie Ray,
Steve

Midwestern Courtesies

My beautiful, loving wife and soulmate, Tracey, is from the Midwest — central Missouri to be exact, a small town on Missouri's Big River. Seems that people in the Midwest have a habit of standing at the door for anywhere between 5 and 30 minutes to say goodbye when leaving a friend's house ... acquaintances too, and store cashiers, and sometimes random people on the street.

There was one time when we were at a holiday cookie-baking party at the house of a friend of a friend — someone I have never spent much time with before this very night. I silently recite my rhyming phrase: *I'm the only Deaf guy here, and everyone is chatting away with holiday cheer.* I usually focus on the food and just keep walking in circles so I don't have to talk to anyone too much. Not because I don't like socializing but because it's just really hard and awkward with the deafness, and most of the time, after a couple hours, I'm just over it.

But all goes well, and I do meet some nice people who write to me when I finally open up and mingle. Yet it's exhausting, and I am ready to go for sure. I check in with Tracey, and she confirms it's time to go. I ask if she is sure about that. "Yes, get the kids and I'll wrap the plates of cookies." So I do my rounds of goodbyes, thanking the hosts, shaking hands, hugging and so on, and I get the kids on "ready when I say so" mode.

So here I am, standing in the entranceway while my beautiful, loving wife and soulmate is saying goodbye to the hosts. It's going on for 15 minutes now and I'm standing there with my coat on, holding two plates of cookies, trying to keep myself busy by making a holiday-type jingle in my head. I sing to myself repeatedly, "Blah, blah, blah-blah, blah. Blah, blah, blah," because although I can't remember or never heard the words, I know the melody. Standing there smiling and nodding whenever they look at me. *Didn't they just do this for three hours on the couch and at the table and at the kitchen counter? Why more now? Tracey said 15 minutes ago, "OK, it's time to go," so I got the coats, shook everyone's hand, got the kids. I put their shoes on, although they are not standing right here in confusion, like their idiot dad. Should I just go and start the car? What are you guys talking about? Maybe I'll get the kids over here and they will piss everyone off somehow and that will remind them we said bye and hugged twice already. What are they talking about? Can you just email later?*

OK, it's definitely getting on 20 minutes now, I'm taking my jacket off and going to fake a bathroom trip and then read that magazine in the den again. The kids are back on the video games downstairs. They intrinsically know the deal and how to make the most of it. They just go maximum pleasure until they are dragged out. *Would it be rude to go to the car? Or go back and check out the DVD library again? Can I get online and watch Netflix? Would that be rude?* I want to do a more thorough check of the garage, a favorite hobby of mine.

What are they talking about? This is so uncomfortably awkward. I hate being in this situation. Please stop looking at me. I'm just going to wait here in the corner by the door. This seems a bit ruder to me, standing here, sulking and silently pressuring my wife to "Just hug them already and let's fucking go!" The kids will come out when we start the car.

Back and forth, we do the little awkward dance around the mudroom. *Are we leaving this time?* I'm kind of hiding behind the big coatrack now. The small group of parents takes a step or two toward the door. I'm totally visual, and it looks like we are going now. *This is it!* I try to help it along by grabbing the doorknob. *This is it! … Nope!* It shifted back to more conversation. *What could they possibly be talking about? Honey, there are more guests in the other room! Let them get back to it. C'mon!?*

The host just sat down on the bench by the entryway, laughing. *Shit.* My wife is laughing, and she keeps looking at me. *Oh shit!*

Don't look at me. Please don't.... "And Steve hurbler Rwanda Kirby dun." *Oh man. Here we go.* I nod and smile. "Jarambe kolooz aye sheerbut dak band, remember that, Steve?" *Are they talking about my old band? Ummmmmmm ... shit. Ask for clarification, fake it, or confuse them with some off-the-wall comment or joke?* "Yeah, kinda. With the band, everything was so busy, it's a little foggy," I say, playing off the band reference. Looks like I'm faking it. I didn't even get a chance to pick; my brain just made the decision for me.

Silence. Everyone is looking confused. I missed it. A bad fake, but understandable after 20 minutes of standing here like an idiot. I should've maybe just asked for clarification. Maybe now we'll just go? Nope. They feel the need to explain, so it's going to be further awkwardness for five minutes of part sign language, part exaggerated lipping and part funny body language to get me to understand that they were talking about that time we ran into each other at the campground years ago, before we actually knew each other. *OK, whew! Holy shit, can we go now?* Nope, got to get the kids' shoes on again and jackets, and we forgot the bowl that we brought the salad in; that's in the kitchen drain board. We all move into the kitchen. They are still talking, and my wife, with her coat still zipped up, sits on the barstool at the kitchen counter as the host reaches for the teapot.

May 12, 2014, 3:10 a.m.

Dear Steve,

Hey man, can you relax a little? I mean, what's the big deal? You can't chill out and be a little confused in the hallway for a half hour? You can't do that for your wife? Figure something out. Like you said, be productive. Make the most of the time. Open up, think around the problem. Maybe there is some technology or something to make these situations better? Maybe just smile and meditate or something. Maybe you can clean out your inbox while you're waiting? Maybe you can communicate about where you're at! "Hey everybody, you know, I can't follow this kind of conversation, so I'm just going to chill out over here and mess around with my phone. No pressure, honey, no problem, I'm good. Take your time."

You can't chill out and deal with this once in a while, for your wife? "Recognize your supports"! Remember that? This woman has been working with you on this for 15 years. You're not the only one affected by the hearing loss. She has been researching, talking to doctors, making all kinds of phone calls and bringing ideas to the table ... with patience, support, smiles, humor and love. Taking on the kids when you're out of it. Birthing the kids for Christ's sake! Gee whiz, man, she learned sign language and repeats things over and over without getting crazed. She interprets for you out in public at all the kids' school events, in restaurants, shopping and every damn place. She never, ever gets upset with you about this stuff. She is so patient with you. She never falters. Always supportive. You are so lucky, man! I tell you one more time, Steve. You need to recognize and show appreciation for your supports.

Peace,
Steve

Concert Fails

I've attended a lot of concerts. Hundreds? A thousand? Everything from bluegrass to jazz, classical, rock, pop and metal. From local singer-songwriters to international sensations. I've spent a lot of money on tickets and actually walked out of close to 50 paid-for concerts ... so far. Why do I keep trying?

The Grateful Dead, RFK Stadium, Washington, D.C., 1990.

I am alone, on the field, in general admission seating. I paid extra in a trade to get on the field this show because about a week ago, I snuck down into the field at the Pittsburgh show and really enjoyed it. Somehow, all contributing factors led to really good sound for me on the field there in Pittsburgh. Whether it was the weather, the humidity, the sound system, my earplugs and earmuffs setup or venue, I was really connecting to the music. It's been off and on at concerts for me for the past year or two. So I got a field ticket for this show and went in really early to get up close to the stage. Mark and the crew have tickets in the stands. Of course no one has cell phones back at this time, so before splitting up, we make plans in the parking lot to meet inside.

Mark says, "Meet at the back of Level 2, Phil's side, at set break."

"Yep. I might go take a break up top, by that orange cone with the construction flag during Drums/Space," I reply. Then we reply in unison, "If all falls through, meet at the van after the show."

Usually either someone in our party is at these predetermined meeting spots or all of us are, and occasionally, no one makes it there. All fine. We always get back to the van. If someone isn't at the van by midnight, we send out the search and rescue. Everyone goes out and looks for the missing person, but I usually go with a partner to make sure I'm hearing the right info from any venue personnel.

Edie Brickell opens the show and the sound is weird, but that's common for opening acts. I just focus on resting physically and mentally for the Dead, coming up later. After checking out a song or two, I plug up with my highest-decibel earplugs and put the muffs on over them, close my eyes and just try to relax and deal with the heat and humidity. It's close to 100 degrees.

A couple of songs in, I get totally sloshed with water. I open my eyes and realize that they got the hoses out and are hosing off the crowd in the field. This is feeling good and I'm glad I plastic-bagged my backup earplugs in my pocket. Wet earplugs do not function well. The moisture changes them, and even if you squeeze them out, usually with moist clothing or even dryer underwear, they still alter the sound negatively compared to a dry pair.

I often get funny looks from the guys checking the bags at the gate as they open my shoulder bag to find a pair or two of earmuffs and various plastic baggies, glasses cases and film containers containing a multitude of fluorescent-colored earplugs. Then there's an empty water bottle that I fill up inside the venue, and a bag of peanuts. I am sober and hydrated and here for the music.

We are waiting for the Dead to start. It's so hot, humid and hazy— people are sweating, lying down in mud and sitting in little puddles. But the energy is high, everyone is smiling and happy and getting psyched for the show. I have three different decibel levels of earplugs with me and a pair of muffs. I figure I will start with my high-grade earplugs that seemed to work in Pittsburgh and see how it goes. The band comes on and it starts raining. The rain feels good, but Jerry isn't looking too good.

I am not really understanding what the opener is. I usually get my cues from the bass because that's my go-to instrument at this

116

stage in my hearing loss. I know most every Dead song and can play most of them but don't know the lyrics and some of the song names. Sometimes I watch people in the crowd singing along to try to get a line on what song it is. Sometimes I'm amazed at the real lyrics to the songs after I read them or am told what they are. I tend to hear the singing as a melody line, not as individual words or sentences.

The first song isn't going well for me, but I decide to leave my protection system as is. The band flows the first song into what I think is Feel Like A Stranger, a tune I know pretty well. *Yep! Stranger! Yay!* But I'm feeling a bit like a stranger right now. I have so much bass going on, I can't get past it to even lock in on the snare drum as I watch Mickey hitting it. Can't pick out any of the guitar, and the keyboards are pretty much nonexistent.

This goes on for another song or two as I move to various positions in the field, trying different spots and different earplugs, and then finally just earmuffs. Nothing is working, and the bass down here on the field is just overbearing. It's vibrating my body and making me sick. I need to try the stands. I'm feeling pretty sick now as I work back to the exit at the far end of the field and start looking for something to throw up in. There's a big, open-top yellow garbage pail, and I hang out there for a few minutes, waiting. Luckily, most of the field crowd is jammed toward the front. There are scattered groups of dancers, twirlers and hoopers back here, which is not making my situation better. Circular motion makes me sick even when I'm standing alone in my room. *What is that even about?* Something about the balance mechanisms and vertigo that I get with the "going deaf" package, I guess. I go over to the pail and vomit a few times, and head up into the stands. People throwing up at Dead shows seems a common occurrence, so I don't think twice about it.

I go on up to a second-level row and shimmy into a free space and check in for a song. *Still sucks.* Still too much bass. I'm not receiving anything from stage right, guitars and keyboard. *Keep moving, man.* I do a circle around the stadium, checking sound and earplug configurations at various spots on the second level with no luck. Still a lot of bass for me and nothing else. Behind the stage is a little better, and I climb up to the highest level of the stadium in hopes for a little more clarity. *Still kinda sucks.* I can't even really tell what song is being played. I am bumming pretty hard. I hang out for a bit and decide to head out to the parking lot before the hallways and stairs get crowded at the set break. *Bummer.* I find a good spot on Shakedown Street, a vending area in the parking lot, and set up our van's grilled cheese stand and get ready to sell some sandwiches after the show.

Rush, MGM Grand Las Vegas, 2004.

This place! Although I've had countless fun moments here, this place really freaks me out. Its overbearing lights, activity and energy rob me of all my senses like an anti-gravity, isolation floatation tank situation. I don't last too long on the Las Vegas Strip, and each visit gets shorter and shorter. Living out West brings us through Vegas once or twice a year as we tour the national parks in the area, go rock climbing at Red Rock Canyon, or go specifically for a certain concert or show.

Mark and I leave the hotel room for the long-awaited, much-appreciated visit with our all-time favorite band, Rush! Even before we get out of the hotel's halls, my senses are depleted as I plug up with medium-grade earplugs at 30 decibels. Auditory communication is out. Getting to the casino level, I'm assaulted by the flashing lights from the machines and neon signs, crowds of people moving in all kinds of random directions or dead-stopping right in front of me. Then there's the multitude of visual oddities that I can't look at for fear of burning out my brain processors trying to understand it all. Visual communication is out.

And people still smoke cigarettes. Even after all the gigs and concerts and everything I've been exposed to through the music industry, I'm still surprised at all the smoke in these places. There's a giant cloud of smoke, and even if I were to get down on my knees and crawl, I couldn't escape it. It dries my eyes out. Visual communication is *totally* out. This smell is not something I am used to, living in the mountains, and my ability to distinguish any smells — or tastes, for that matter, other than cigarette smoke — is destroyed. Olfactory and gustatory support is out. That leaves me with touch, and I am not touching anything on the germ-ridden Las Vegas Strip.

I walk two paces directly behind Mark, with my eyes down, and just follow his feet through the casino to the street. This is even worse. Higher-intensity flashing lights, noises, screaming, laughing, car engines, crowds, some beggars and solicitors, with a side order of drunkards. *Just follow Mark. Watch his feet. Don't look up. Ugh! This place!* I can handle this stuff and have navigated through this alone many times, but I'm trying to conserve brain-processing energy for the show.

We get to the MGM arena, where the search crew lady smiles at me and shows me that her earplugs are already in after she inspects my bag and finds all my earplug canisters.

We are pretty pumped up for this show. It's been a while since I went to a concert with Mark, and I finally agreed to come along on this one. We grew up listening to Rush. Like most Rush fans, I could air-drum, air-guitar, bass and keys through every Rush song from the first album until *Presto*, their 14th studio album, when my hearing got too bad to access new material. Mark could air-play the entire Rush collection and *play* it on bass as well.

Our seats are on the first level off the floor, directly opposite the stage. We are hanging out writing notes back and forth on my pad as we wait for the show to start. We realize we are veterans here now and are glad to see a bunch of teens and 20-year-olds in attendance.

It's time. The lights dim and Alex and Geddy come out waving while Neil gets behind the drum set. They kick off into what I'm guessing is a song, but from my experiences up to this point, I'm sensing that this is an Ultra Extreme Volume Situation, which to me sounds like a crunching, rhythmic jet engine. I am not able to even distinguish a rhythm. I see that Geddy is on the keyboards and I'm hoping it's something from the recent years, one of the songs that I am not too familiar with. I was expecting problems, but not so severe. I look at Mark, who's smiling.

"What song is this?" I lip and sign to him.

"Subdivisions," he lips back.

Damn. I know this. I know every note of this. I've played this. I listened to this on a radio beneath my pillow late at night for a week when they put it out as a single before they released the album in 1982. A friend of mine made me a cassette tape of just Subdivisions playing over and over for 60 minutes. *Damn.*

I try to focus but can't get to any point of recognition. The second song starts, and it's the same. I look at Mark and shake my head a little. He nods apologetically and signs "large amount" and "money" for the song The Big Money. He knows what's going on. I try to add the muffs over the plugs for the next couple of songs, but it's just a mess. I don't want to bum him out, so I decide to split. I give him a high-five and sign "noise" and "me-up." He knows I'm going to try to check out sound situations in the upper levels and around the arena before leaving.

Some other notable concerts I walked out of: Peter Gabriel, King Crimson, Phish, Bela Fleck and the Flecktones, George Benson and my son's middle school band performance. Why do I keep trying?

June 26, 2014, 1:14 a.m.

Dear Steve,

Yeah, that sucks, maybe you can get some money back from Ticketmaster! Ha ha. Dude! You left a Halloween Phish show!? Hey man, bummer, but you did get to experience a lot of music and concerts and watch some of the masters, you know? Some people never get any of that. You've been extraordinarily lucky, man! How about thinking about and remembering all the concerts you DID see and experience? You're sounding a little negative here. Stay positive, man. Those were some good times. Not to mention, once you stopped going to concerts, didn't you discover another type of artistic performance in Vegas? Those Cirque du Soleil shows you started going to when you couldn't hear the music anymore. Right?! Those are awesome! There's little to no talking, they are a visually communicated concept show, and international, so specific language isn't used! What a discovery! From Cirque to dance, magic shows to Blue Man Group type stuff. Didn't this trigger a lot of creation for you with your black-light videos, and art lessons in school?

Dude. One door closes, another opens.

Stay positive,
Steve

Movie Fails

I've gone to a lot of movies as well. Maybe more movies than concerts! In the past decade, since they started providing captioning devices, I have walked out of exactly 19 of 34 movies, as of this publish date. I've kept track on a little note in my wallet. That's more walkouts than stay-ins. Why do I keep trying?

Through middle school, I would probably go once a week. I would save my chores money for tickets or at least to pay for popcorn. I always hold the popcorn.

In high school, I had a good amount of cash on hand from working a few different jobs. I averaged probably twice a week. Once a week at the multiplex for the new arrivals, and once at the dollar cinema as a social event with all my friends. My friends usually got, or snuck in, candy and soda, but I always got popcorn for the crunching effect.

Through college and my early 20s, I averaged a few times a month, maybe less. Money was tighter because I was on my own, ticket prices increased, and hearing and comprehension decreased drastically. I was experiencing movies at a different level than the director intended. I was making up my own stories while watching their visuals. I usually just attended for the social aspect, hanging out with friend groups. I felt loss, missing my cinema experiences, but I was playing a lot of music at this time, and my focus and attention were elsewhere.

Then I stopped going to the movies for about 10 years as DVDs and captioned movies became more available at home. This worked out pretty well until I exhausted the library of captioned videos. Captioning wasn't easy to come by. When I was younger, I would get really angry because not all movie rentals had captions! I would write letters to studios and production companies and sometimes send them and sometimes not.

It's cool talking about this with Deaf and hard-of-hearing friends now because we all had this experience as the industry adapted and transitioned to trying to caption its media. Things got a lot better and FCC laws were put into effect to caption all TV and produced media by 20-whatever, and updates were made to the Communications Act. Everything was getting better for the Deaf and hard-of-hearing community around captioning until ... YouTube. No captions, automatic captioning, self-made captions, joke captioning, and a lot of confusion for me around YouTube. I missed a lot of good stuff, for sure, but that's the way it goes sometimes.

I remember the day Mark said, "Dude, this movie theater in Springfield has some sort of captioning glasses. You can wear these glasses at the big screen and it captions them somehow!"

"Really, like Geordi on Star Trek or something? Hell yeah! Let's go!" In 2013, Regal Cinema developed a captioning device that allows the viewer to see captions as they would be accessed at home, through these special glasses that can be worn over regular glasses, and they even have a 3-D adaptation. We actually went to Star Trek Into Darkness for my first captioned big-screen movie! It worked! I watched the movie and read the captions right in front of me through these glasses that no one else could see. It was very liberating.

I'm back!... and I'm holding the popcorn! Tracey thinks I like crunching because it's some type of tactile, sensory deaf thing. I can't hear the crunching, so I very dramatically crunch and munch popcorn so that I can *feel* it, and apparently, so can the people sitting near me.

Soon after the glasses, another theater in my area introduced a captioning device that fits into the cup holder on your seat. Whoa! Two choices to choose from. Soon most theaters had most movies listed as closed-captioning accessible and I started to attend movies almost as often as I used to when I was a kid.

As with any new technology, there are going to be issues to overcome. With the glasses, there's the pain and piercing sting into the side of your head for two-plus hours. There's the need to get there early and sit in the middle of the theater, so the glasses don't project the captions onto the side wall. With both, there's what we call the occasional "tech failure." Where it just isn't f-ing working.

Then, with the cup-holder device, there's the "screw's not tight" issue and the unit is floating around for two hours where I have to have one hand holding it while I jam the popcorn bucket between my leg and the seat so I can eat it all with my other hand. I've started to bring a small monkey wrench to movies to tighten the bottom nut on that sucker!

There's the "if you want to go in, get a seat, and then go get popcorn, you're out of luck" issue. You can't really go anywhere near your specific theater or else the device registers your presence and clicks "ON." Then if you exit the vicinity, the device gets confused and shuts off or picks up another movie's captions. So I go to the bathroom and fill my water bottle on the other side of the building before the movie begins and then go to my specific theater. You have to go in and sit down, send your wife to get popcorn, and stay there and hope it works after the previews, which aren't captioned. Occasionally, there's also the aforementioned tech failure, when it just isn't f-ing working.

It's the tech failures that screw me up the most. As I said, 19 out of 34 times, according to my records, there have been tech failures, where the movie starts but the captions don't. So, I sit with my friends or family for five or so minutes after the movie starts, messing with the buttons on the unit because no captions are being produced, get pissed, then take a bunch of deep breaths and go to acceptance, and let my wife or child or friend know that "Shit's fucked up, I'll catch the next one." I leave the popcorn and go to the service desk to let them know in niceties that "Shit's fucked up," and they give me redeemable tickets for future presentations. I go and meditate out front, or get a beer, or walk around, or drive around, or go home.

It can be disappointing, but overall, I'm so grateful for technology right now and for this advancement in accessibility for us at the cinema. I know it's going to get better and better. I'm psyched!

June 12, 2014, 4:02 a.m.

Dear Steve,

I love your positive attitude here, man! Awesome. You should get involved in developing better technology for the Deaf and hard of hearing. You have a lot of ideas, man! You have that list of really cool stuff for movie theaters, concerts, social situations, restaurants … while you're at it, you should get involved with advocating for captioning and access to media in your school district. Set a meeting with the district offices to talk to them about captioning the district's Professional Development courses, because remember that one last year? It sucked! It was so boring because their videos weren't captioned. You were left out. Baloney! Set that shit straight, Steve. It's an awareness thing, man! They're not oppressing you on purpose. They just don't *know* yet. They don't understand. They have a lot of stuff to deal with, man. You've got to let them know!

Dude … thanks,
Steve

Teaching

It took a while to find my path, but as it turned out, I found I had a knack for working with kids, and teaching and learning by experiential means seemed to be my specialty. This is also a great way for special-needs kids to learn. I built, from scratch, a Deaf education program at a small district high school and then was called back to rejuvenate the program a few years later. Other schools in the district tapped me to help fix and build their Deaf education programs. I currently teach at a high school near my house, and classes are very successful. I also have time to continue writing, recording and performing music. So things did seem to work out professionally, and I am helping kids.

<u>Helping Them</u>

Years ago, I was teaching Deaf Education at a suburban high school outside a major city. We had a new student join the class in the middle of the year. The student, Raul, had just moved to the area with his family from Mexico. He is profoundly Deaf. He had no spoken English, no ASL, no Spanish Sign Language. Just some "home signs" and organized gestures that he used with family and friends, and some written Spanish knowledge. He was 13 when he came to our school.

To my surprise, the school supported me in giving us an hour a day of one-on-one time. I had this kid an hour a day and a whole empty room! Because he had no language, everything was a learning experience. We did a lot. I found out that he was into cars and motorcycles and motors. So I decided to get the stuff to repair an old motor of mine, order parts online and build a scooter ... all the while teaching Raul ASL, English vocabulary, language use, grammar, communication skills, how to fill out forms, letter writing, blah, blah, blah, and all that important school stuff. I was psyched! We were building a scooter! We got the motor in one

131

day, and let me tell you, this kid knows tools and engines and how they work and what they need. He doesn't have the language to express it, but he knows. He "took me to school" with the motor and the building of the scooter, that's for sure. Nobody ever bothered us, and we did this for a whole semester. In the spring we rolled it out into the empty lot, started it up and ran it around a bunch. It was cool. Kids came out to see and took pictures.

We both learned a lot. I still talk to Raul. He is a successful mechanic in his town. He got married and is thinking about having kids. We went snowboarding recently, and he told me that was a special time for him, when we built that scooter and he learned ASL, and learned how to learn. He thanked me for that. I am helping kids.

One high school I worked at asked me to teach a few Special Education classes with hearing kids to fill the schedule. This situation was challenging for me. I had to establish different communication methods with individual students because they all communicate differently. Some can't speak clearly, some don't make eye contact, some can't write clearly, and so on. *What am I doing in here?* Well, this also seemed to work out, and we had a lot of fun after they got to know me and we became comfortable with each other's needs.

There was one 10th-grade student, Alisha, whom I worked with on math. Every day, math problem after math problem. You get to know someone really well after a few thousand math problems and all the freak-outs, math jokes and broken pencil points that accompany them. So one day I noticed she wasn't looking too good. Next day the same. Looking depressed. This carried on for a week or two. I was asking questions like, "What's up?" "You OK?" "What's going on?" "Boys?" All the usual nosy teacher stuff. Finally, one day, she kind of tears up and tells me she is really depressed, like "*bad* depressed." Things are looping around in her head, over and over.

So I'm kind of freaked out, a bit scared, and I'm just thinking to tell her good stuff, be positive, tell her how awesome she is, and I grab an index card and draw a picture of a cat on it. I write in math jargon, "Alisha = really cool girl. Alisha = pretty + smart. Creative + funny. Alisha = clever + cute like a cat." (She is really into cats.) She laughed a little, and I sent her over to the counselor.

Her mood seemed to get a little better that week, and after a month or two, back to normal. We became good friends and had a few more classes over the years. Sometime around her graduation, she asked me if I remembered that year when she was in my Academic Support class. She said that was a bad year for her and she was cutting herself. She took out the old index card from her bag and told me that she kept it and she reads it when she is feeling bad. She said it helped her stop cutting that year. I am helping kids.

<u>Helping Me</u>

One day Raul asked me how old I was, and I told him I was 32. He made an exaggerated, crunched-up "sorry" face and jokingly signed "Soon, dead, you!" We laughed, but I was a little freaked out. *Whoa!* It bothered me the whole night, but when I woke the next morning, I realized what a gift he gave me. I don't want to die anytime soon, I'm not expecting to anytime soon, but most definitely will at some point, probably sooner than Raul. After accepting this fact, I felt free! Free from the fear of trying new things, free from the fear of embarrassment or failure. If I just live for the day, who cares about that stuff? I made a poster with the slogan "SOON-DEAD-YOU" and hang it in every classroom I've worked in since that time with Raul. New classes ask about it every year, and I get to talk about the freedom Raul gave me through acceptance. What a gift!

I had one particular student for three years straight. Every day, after class, she told me, "Thanks, have a good day." Every day for three years. We never joked about it. Most days I was so caught up in class and all the craziness, trying to catch my breath, thinking about the next class, that it was a surprise when she approached to remind me to have a nice day.

Then there was a student of mine who got a cochlear implant when she was a baby, and it's working out pretty well for her after a lot of training. When I was struggling one time with my hearing loss, she told me, "Loosen up, Steve. You get what you get. You know? Have fun with it. You can do it."

Any teacher can tell you that sometimes you just lose your shit—trying to do a lesson while the kids are talking, text-messaging, fooling around—you just start to lose it. I work with a lot of students with multiple disabilities. I had a student with Down syndrome in ASL class for two years. During a lesson, lecture or activity, this girl would see me or sense me starting to flip out, come up and give me a hug and pat my back. The rest of the class eventually figured out what was going on and supported us, regrouping and getting on with the lesson.

I have endless stories about the kids I've worked with over the years. I could fill volumes about our stories together and the gifts they give me every day. Their humor, attention and knowledge. Their quirks, their stories and their faults. Their fears, their successes and their love.

February 2, 2014, 3:34 a.m.

Dear Steve,

Don't forget, you ended up in this field because of your deafness. Being deaf opened doors that you would not have even knocked on. It gave you a perspective on things you never would have seen, and experiences you never would have experienced. What a great job you have! You get the opportunity to help kids, and they get the opportunity to help you. You are so lucky!

It took a while, but you found a skill you can build on. You worked with what you have, and you built on it. Everyone has gifts and skills. You found yours and worked it. You still have some undiscovered skills, man. Find them and work the heck out of them. Work it from the right, from the left, take it apart and rebuild it. Throw it far away and look at it from that point of view. Way across the street, across the field, across the city, in a different country. Break it down and eat it, take a little nibble every hour and suck on it for the whole hour, for a whole day. Look at it from that point of view. You have skills! You're special, man! Maybe it's with food, maybe it's with animals, maybe numbers, maybe crayons, computers, speaking, machines or magnifying glasses. You have a specialness about you. Find more of it, Steve. Try new things. Open up, reorganize and observe the many assets you have and what you can do with them. It doesn't have to be one or the other. It is all available for you. Recognize your gifts and give praise! Thank someone. It's a gift! Whoever it is you want to thank—your God, your community, your mother or father, your family, your friend.

Thank them, then thank yourself, Steve, because ultimately, you're the one who was present and accepted the gift, opened the gift and realized it. You're the one who worked on making it better, and you're the one who is going to keep working on becoming better. You're the one who will share it with others.

Thank you,
Steve

Awkward

<u>The Restaurant</u>

To Deaf people, sometimes it seems like hearing people have a special power of disappearing and reappearing. One time my class played a trick on me. I was doing a lesson and writing some instructions on the board, and when I turned around, the room was empty. They'd snuck out while my back was turned. They planned it, and it worked perfectly.

There is this second or two of shock and surprise before your deaf brain remembers it's deaf! Sometimes I'm talking to someone and turn around to grab something, and turn back, and they're gone! Vanished to the other side of the room. "Oh, there you are. OK, what was I saying?" Hearing people seem to pop up from the ground, vanish, reappear, walk through walls—it's kind of magical to my deaf brain. So I always try to sit with my back to the wall or stand in a corner and scan my current environment for changes, processing anything that can give context to what is about to be said, heard or discussed.

In restaurants, I joke around with my wife that I need to sit in the corner seat in case we get attacked by ninjas, but in reality, it's so that hearing people can't do their magic voodoo on me. By sitting in a corner of a room and being able to see everyone and everything, I can prepare myself, notice who might be coming over, try to figure out who it is, gather information about the situation and develop context of what might be said and what I might need to "hear." *Be prepared!* The Boy Scout motto!

Nobody really likes surprise "Hello" visits when you're at a romantic restaurant with your spouse, right? Picture this. You're having a nice, quiet dinner with your spouse whom you haven't talked to in two months because you have two toddlers. You finally get out, and you're both relaxing. She is relaxed and signing well and sometimes writing cute little notes just for you!

Things are going smoothly with the communication with the waiter, and the orders are spot-on. The main course comes, and you're really getting into your chicken dish. Cutting a nice juicy end piece off the bone there, really working it. It's going to be great. There's a little bit of fat on there, the perfect amount of Française sauce and two whole capers. You bring the fork to your mouth, and as you take that first bite, you look up, and there's your ex from college shaking hands with your wife and seating herself at the empty chair. They start chatting about something you can't hear. So you keep eating and smiling and nodding. Awkward!

Barns

I like old broken-down barns. I think I like that they make me remember an old house on my father's land that my family used to visit when we were younger. I live in the Rocky Mountain foothills and go hiking frequently and see a lot of old barns and get to reminiscing.

When I'm out on a hike, I always walk on the very right side of the trail. It's become such a habit that it's almost an obsession now. I don't think about it, but subconsciously, I'm stuck on the right side. If I stop, it's on the right side. Need to pee, I find myself heading into the bushes on the right side. Stop to look at a barn? I step off to the right side. I've found there's a safety issue with being Deaf and crossing the middle line. Sometimes the trail becomes a one-lane footpath and I turn to check behind me every 10 or 20 steps. But it never fails. Every once in a while, I get caught up in my thoughts, and BAM! A biker or jogger swerves around me through the grasses or bushes. Without a thought I just yell, "Sorry, I'm Deaf. Didn't hear ya."

So one time, with an old barn across the creek, I step off the trail to the right and look at the barn for a bit, remembering my dad and the old house. After a few minutes, I feel something next to me, turn, and BAM! I let out a startled "Ahhhhrg!" at the sudden magical appearance of a 30-something-year-old jogger lady standing next to me. A little out of breath, she says, "Flargau booter darn undergru — ette jarnut."

"What? Sorry," I say, pointing to my ears. "I'm Deaf."

"Oh, ummmm…. Never mind." Of course I can read that part easily. She turns and jogs away. Awkward!

<u>Trees in the Wind</u>

One of my favorite things to see are the leaves of a big tree fluttering in the wind. The abstract chaos, the patterns and the shifts in color tone. Another time out on a hike, from the right side of the trail, I'm watching the leaves do their dance on a big cottonwood. I'm getting mesmerized and into the leaf trance, staring intently. I break free, turn around, and BAM! The magical appearance of a group of eight or so YMCA kids and their staff leader standing there behind me. Looking up at the tree, looking at me, looking to the tree, to me, back and forth.

I smile and raise my hand in the typical open-hand wave. I look back to the tree, look back at them and notice one kid is doing the "sh" sign with his index finger to another kid. Most are looking at the tree.

The group leader leans over to me and whispers, "Sh z wh sss skls ess wswsw."

"Sorry, I am Deaf, say again?" I whisper back.

The leader nods and acts out a "That's cool. No problem" gesture. All of the kids are staring at me now but trying to act like they aren't looking. One superhero kid steps out a little and mouths a big giant "Oh" and starts miming a bird, making big wings with his arms and then pointing at the tree. Starting to comprehend the situation, I look at the tree and back and shake my head "no." He then starts acting like a mountain lion, doing claws with his hands and a silent roar with his mouth, looking at the tree and pointing with the eyebrows-up-question face. Instead of trying to explain to the group of 8-year-olds how I like to zone out on the cosmic patterns of the leaves in the breeze, I decide to fake it and play along and get the heck out of here. I shake my head "no" again and make the owl sign by drawing circles around my eyes and big wings with my arms and mouthing "hoot, hoot." Then show it flying away and wave bye to it. The kid nods and smiles. The staff leader nods and smiles and I head off. Awkward, but fun.

Under Houses

After college and moving to the Rocky Mountain region, I started a handyman business rather than going for a service or office job. I picked up a few clients, and by word of mouth, became full-time. Even now, 20 years later, I still do jobs in between my teaching schedule.

One particular plumbing job found me down in the crawl space under a residential house in the suburbs. This starts off by finding the access panel out behind the house under shrubs, pricker bushes and old garbage that gets blown into that scary corner of the yard where nobody goes. Then I need to pry off that panel, which usually falls apart somehow because of rot or poor construction. I remove the access panel and prop it against the house in its semi-broken state, realizing I'll need to fix this too or build a new one.

I look down into the hole filled with cobwebs like the fake stuff you put around the door and trees on Halloween. I get a long curved stick from the yard, clear away what I can, grab the toolbox and descend into the entrance pit. Without touching the moldy, mucky, mildew crud growing on the cement surrounding me, I spark my headlamp and peer into the desolate emptiness ahead. I take stock. It is about 3.5 feet of headspace, a dirt floor, a few pipes visible, a few wires hanging, some old … what is that? … a pile of unidentifiable house stuff that's rusting out to the point of deterioration, and loads and loads of cobwebs. I decide to put my dust mask on for this one, and just as I wrap the rubber band around the back of my head, a giant alien-moth bounces off my face and flutters past and out of sight.

So, I make it over to the section of the house where the plumbing is that I need to repair and spend five minutes clearing out a 6 ft. radius to create a relatively web-less, spider-less, other creature-less work zone. Even up in the rafters above my head. Especially in the rafters, where those weirdo insects dwell. That's why you want to have a curved stick — to get the crud out of the rafters above you without it all falling in your face.

After I acclimate to the environment, the work starts and seems to be going smoothly as I get more focused. Working on a section of pipe, I sense a shadow flutter across the stream of light created by the entryway hole. I come down from the work inside that rafter, back to my sitting-rest position, and sense something behind me. I turn around, and BAM! Magically, someone has appeared in the crawl space between my work area and the entryway. I shine my headlamp in that direction, and coming toward me, on all fours, dragging something behind him, is ... Hagrid? *Holy shit!* He slowly crawls closer and closer. It's a giant guy, with a massive Hagrid mustache and beard and a winter cap, dragging a bag of ...? Bones? Children's fingers? Magical creatures? *Oh crap.*

I'm not a big person, and whenever I do these jobs in confined spaces, I wonder how those big worker-type guys are able to manage these spaces. But here comes Hagrid's brother or cousin, and he really is big. His facial hair alone must weigh 10 pounds. He is right on top of me now, taking up a large amount of space and situating himself into a kneeling, half-sitting, leaning position. I can't see his lips through the beard and mustache. I say "Hi," and he says something — about six or seven words of something — and drags his sack over. I still can't see the bag — it's still behind him, his massive frame blocking my sight line. He turns a bit and rummages through the bag and starts to pull something out. *Oh shit! What's it going to be? A crowbar? A couple dead bunnies? A sandwich?*

Out of the bag, he pulls another bag. A black canvas bag about the size of a loaf of bread. He turns to me and starts talking and offers his hand. I shake, hesitantly, and it feels like I'm shaking hands with a baseball mitt. There's no possible chance of reading this guy's lips with the facial hair and the headlamp, so I pull myself together and say, "I'm Deaf, I can't see your lips, please don't kill me." Thinking … *Who the hell are you? What are you doing down here? And that black cloth bag must have surgical tools to torture me with, so if you go for it, I'm going to smack you in the head with the blowtorch tank.*

He starts laughing, a big jolly-Santa type laugh, and from the sack pulls out a battery lantern unit. He turns it on and it really brightens up the scene down there. I can see his eyes better now, and I start to relax a bit, in light of the kind eyes and the Santa laugh.

He's still chuckling and says, "Grumble, grumble-grumble, grumble, grumble-grumble, grumble, grumble, grumble, grumble, grumble-grumble-grumble, grumble." I can barely see his mouth moving. I can't distinguish the number of words or even if he is done speaking. Just hair moving. He could be chewing gum — or bunny rabbit ears.

"No, sorry, I am Deaf and I can't read your lips. Do you have a paper and pen?"

He tries again with more mouth exaggerations. "Grumble, grumble-grumble, grumble, grumble-grumble, grumble, grumble-grumble-grumble, grumble. Grumble, grumble-grumble, grumble, grumble-grumble." Then he smiles with raised eyebrows like it was a question.

I'm sucking in the air through my teeth and shaking my head slightly the whole while he's grumbling. I say "Nope, I am just not getting it. I have no idea what you're saying. I can't read your lips. Hmmmm…. maybe we can draw in the dirt, or….?"

He moves the lantern between us and pulls up his mustache. His lip goes up a ways too, and I have images of snarling dogs and grinning ogres. His teeth look pretty clean though — no bunny flesh — and he tries again. "Grrrrrraa grra gara raa grrrrrraa grra gara raa, grrrrrraa grra gara raa. Grrrrrraa grra-gara-raa?" Definitely a question with the eyebrows up at the end and tilted head. He looks at me knowing that this didn't work either, and his body slumps a little with disappointment.

That was a pretty good effort, and I'm feeling more comfortable. "Shit man, I am really sorry. I just can't figure out what is going on."

He slowly puts up the "Hold it, I got an idea" finger, opens the black canvas bag and takes out a video camera. He points it at the pipes above my head and makes the old-time "camera rolling" signal with his other hand.

He wants to take a picture of the work for insurance? He wants to film a cute plumber guy in the crawlspace working? He wants to film creepy insects? This has actually just become a better situation for me as we move into me asking yes-or-no questions, and the guy just shaking his head or nodding. I start with, "You want to take pictures for insurance?" He shakes his head no and does the film signal again. I decide to skip the second idea and ask, "You want to film spiders and insects?" He shakes his head no and points to the pipes. I then ask, "You want to film the pipes. You want to film me working on the pipes for insurance?" He does the "kind-of" thing with his hand, like a balance. The classic "so-so" signal. He does the film signal again and slaps his chest a few times. Film signal, slap chest, slap chest. Then he mimics leaving and looking at the camera, doing the thinking and scratching his beard thing while nodding and pointing to his head repeatedly like he's "getting it."

"You want to film the repair?" He nods. Smiling eyes.

I think I'm getting it. "You want to film the repair and watch it later?" He nods excitedly.

Joking now, "You want to film the repair and watch it later with your wife?" He shakes his head no, taps his chest and points to his head a few times, which reminds me of the sign for "thinking."

"You want to film the repair. You want to watch it later? You want to learn how to do the repair!? Watch it later!" He roars some

147

Viking-sounding salute and puts up the baseball glove hand for a high five. *Holy shit.* We high-five.

OK, I'm relaxed now and shift it over to teaching mode. I set up the space and go through the steps for a half-inch copper pipe section repair. I talk him through it as I do it, and he nods a lot and I can see the smiling eyes. He just stays and films one or two sections and then gives me a few big pats on the shoulder, packs up the camera and light, then a few more pats, and then a few more before he waves and crawls on out. I finish up the job and go up to see the client. He apologizes for forgetting to tell me that his brother-in-law wanted to learn how to repair a burst copper pipe and would be joining me with his camera to film some of the repair for reference purposes. I said that was fine and that we had fun down there. Kind of fun at the end there, but the lead-in was awkward. Totally awkward.

May 17, 2014, 3:03 a.m.

Dear Steve,

Listen man, you have a very vivid imagination. Remember, awkward to you is often not awkward to others. Steve, you need to have a pen and paper with you at all times. "Be prepared," the Boy Scout motto. You're an Eagle Scout, man! You carry your wallet all the time in your front pocket, right? Cut the crap and put a little mini-pencil in there and a few small sheets of paper. That's it, done.

Boy Scout salute!

Love,
Steve

Audiologist Report

<u>Hearing Status</u>: Severe to profound hearing loss. Bilateral, sensorineural. Approximately 85 percent loss in the left ear and 90 percent loss in the right ear.

<u>Hyperacusis</u>: High sensitivity to loud, sharp sounds.

<u>Tinnitus</u>: Tinnitus holding steady as a high-pitched white noise at about 30 percent blanket over the residual hearing. Post-surgery tinnitus escalation.

<u>Notes</u>: Not using hearing aids because there isn't much to amplify.

Death by Prius or Biker Mob

Mark and I joke that I'm either going to get struck down on my longboard by not hearing a hybrid vehicle coming around the turn of my street doing 35 mph, or I'll be beaten to death by a biker gang.

Along with the hearing loss, I have the sensitivity problem, hyperacusis. Most loud noises throw me for a little brain zap. Like an electric shocker to the head. It feels physical, like someone is poking me in the inner ear. My brother has the same issue, as I'm sure a lot of other people do too. Sharp noises such as dishes clanging, electric tools, kids banging on stuff, babies screaming. Stuff like that, and … motorcycles.

Most of my life, I've been building up this frustration with motorcyclists and the muffler issue. I would really like to spend some time communicating with any random motorcyclist about the bikes, the engine systems and the exhaust system, and really just come to an understanding on the question of "Why the hell can't you put a muffler on the exhaust pipe, you asshole?"

I have a bad habit of flipping off bikers as they ride past me when I'm on the sidewalk. So here I am, trying to protect myself from the obnoxiousness coming down the street, with my pinkie in one ear and my head tilted onto my other shoulder, blocking that ear, so my arm is free to fly the big throbbing middle finger to the guy as he passes by. Women too, I don't give a shit. Sometimes I can't get it together fast enough and I just cover my ears with both hands and stick out my tongue and inch my way out into the street, gyrating my privates so they're sure to see me.

One time I half-mooned a guy and then totally ran away a few blocks because it was still kind of light out, just as dusk was approaching. Another time I gave a big two-handed flip-off to an oncoming trio of bikes with riders on the back. A double pump flip-off, one for each, with corresponding "FUCK," "FUCK,"

"FUCK" (mouthed, not yelled). Looking back, that could've been the beating, but I always seem to be in middle-class suburban settings. So, it's probably just a bunch of older recreational bikers out for their Sunday ride. Regardless, I have a little bit of a problem, and I can't seem to get over it. I even flip off emergency vehicle sirens and passing trains.

One time my wife and kids caught me flipping off a biker as we were walking through town on our way to get some dinner. My beautiful, loving wife and soulmate, Tracey, took the mother role and said something along the lines of, "That's totally inappropriate, don't ever do that again. Ever!" My daughter, like most 7-year-old kids with their parents out in public, just starts kicking me whenever I do anything outside the norm of "walking quietly like a completely normal person." Even if I sing a little tune or just hum something … kick! If I jump over a puddle and then do a little two-step jig after … kick! My 10-year-old son doesn't seem to care — we sometimes act weird in the street for fun — so he probably thought it was part of that game.

Regardless, I have a bit of a problem and it's a bad model for the kids, right? I am working on it, and a few times after writing the first draft of this chapter, I began holding my ears, taking deep breaths and smiling at the passing bikers. I still stare them down and probably have the creepy-smiling-lunatic-face happening, but it might save me a beating.

August 9, 2014, 1:03 a.m.

Dear Steve,

This is your problem, not other people's. Don't load your problem onto others. Everybody's got their own problems to deal with; they don't need yours. You need to work on your problem and make adjustments in your life to deal with it. If you need to wear earplugs whenever you go out into town, then that is what you need to do. You can't expect the world to change for you and your problems. Be prepared, right?

Stata-ten.

Love,
Steve

Holy-Shit Lady

In the produce section at the supermarket: *Two red peppers, garlic, onions ... two red peppers, garlic, onions ... Ooooh, nice vine tomatoes! ... Two red peppers ... OK, maybe these shallots instead of the onion...*

Ah! Oooooooh, no.

Who's that? She is looking at me; she knows me? She looks familiar? No. Shit. She is making the "Hey! I know you" raised-eyebrow-greeting thing right to me. She is coming right at me. Am I smiling? Oh shiiiiiiit! Fortyish-year-old woman coming at me. Could be a friend of my wife, could be one of my kids' friends' mothers. Oh shit. Am I smiling? I think I'm smiling and doing the raised-eyebrow thing back. Could be a neighbor or an old client. Oh man ... shit! Could be a mother of one of my students! I have my garage-cleaning clothes on; I just ran out to get some stuff to make chili later. She is like 8 feet away and closing in now, rounding the sweet potatoes, and she is definitely going to say something to me.

"Hi," I say first, kind of pensive. Looks like I'm going to try to play this like I know who it is, and take the offense. I didn't even tell myself to do it. I just did it.

"I, −o−, −t, −ere−ungle −i−a-, nutter-jimbo," she says with a real nice big smile.

Oh man. No chance at that one. Hold on the identification issue and deal with the nutter-jimbo issue.

I suck in air through my teeth to show that I'm flustered and say, "Sorry?" and point to my ear and shake my head.

" −ed um− flabbu-cry, ah kind-r − manu− k− − sharona!" she says with a real nice big smile.

Sharona? Like the song My Sharona? "Ooooh you make my motor run, my motor run...." What is she saying? She can't be talking about that 70s song. This is bad. I can't make out one word. I'm starting to sweat. Was that band called The Knack? She does have a nice, genuine smile for me. She must know me and know I'm Deaf. What's a Sharona? I'm wondering if that is even the right word to the song. Shit.

I do the eyebrows-raised-and-nod-my-head-like-I-understood thing and say "Yeah." *Oh crap!*

Did you just say "Yeah"? What an idiot! Dude, you're trying to fake through this one?

She smiles bigger and nicer now. "T—nee eh kouledger—n drahker eyeee, kouledger—fn d—ng klump tood—y wazzer doon wazzer together—urt myopau."

This is bad. Bad! Maybe if she stopped with the smiling I could read her lips. Shit. Shit. Shit. I think she said something about "together" or putting things together, or togetherness. This has got to be a parent of one of my students. Who the hell is this? She looks a little like....? NOBODY! I have no idea who this is. What is she "putting together"? If I can figure that out....

NO! Don't fake it, man! You got to lay it down. Come clean.

I do the slow exhale thing while squeezing my chin with a confused face. "I just ... I don't understand, sorry."

Now she's nodding, still with the big smile. "d—e—oit mutter—, —ter-ah kind-r—, —glibly to go together sheeper— knoon bigboo, —aye—ee—t ma-te j—dah , flumper draken—eye rounder *(I'm going to puke!)* —nk lasten humpter gonna shirt mastic. *(Who is this lady?)* Raskn zephine —nike datsun beli-watton itty. Gone zephyr toon? Gone zephyr Toon also?"

Holy shit. Oh my God. Oh. My. God. Don't say "Yeah," Steve. Do not even nod. Dude! Don't fake this one! You're in a hole now, man, but you can do this. Breathe. Come clean. Go clean with her on this.

This is so awkward and I am totally sweating. Does she see that I am sweating? I don't have my paper and pen. I don't even have my phone with the voice-to-text thingy. She is still smiling. I'm going to drop my basket and run out of here. Holy shit!

All I say is "No ... no," shaking my head again and pointing to my ear. Moving my gaze off her lips and making eye contact with her now.

Taking a little off the smile, she inclines her body toward me a little. "d— —e —oit mutter—, — —ter ah kind-r —, —glibly to go together sheeper —knoon bigboo, —aye—ee—t ma-te j—dah , flumper draken—eye rounder —nk lasten humpter gonna shirt mastic. *(Oh my god, she is repeating the same thing word for word. Holy shit, lady! Come on!)* Raskn zephine —nike datsun beli-watton -itty. Gone zephyr toon? Beyonce zephyr toon also?"

Beyonce? The singer? No way. Fuck this. Ummmmmmm…. OK. She is not getting it. Does she know me? Does she know I'm Deaf? If she's a student's mom, she must know. My wife's friend, she must know. If we met before, she must know. Who are you, lady? Holy shit! Am I getting hit on? No way. Maybe she is just asking about the damn vegetables or something about the store.

"I don't understand. I can't read your lips. I'm sorry." Relieved that I came clean. In another situation I would probably joke around about her lips being too fabulous and distracting for lip-reading, but I'm totally off-kilter.

"Zanube —tu aye —ur—on danter cranus —per, together vabid peter?" Smiling.

Holy shit lady! What the hell? This is freaking me out. Please stop the creepy smiling! I'm going to run.

"Sorry, I just don't understand." Pleading now. Hands out and palms up and open. Shaking my head.

"Noodus wanna donner —eppa —aye colundron? Lister —y modusin donner —eppa?" Smiling. She's leaning more forward.

"Sorry." Pointing to my ear and making the "I suck" face, the "I am disappointed in myself" face. *I need to get the hell out of here right now. I'm going to start crying and maybe puke. Holy shit! My tummy is getting all queasy. Right now. I should just drop the basket and run.*

"Lister — —y modusin donner —eppa?" Smiling.
Ho-ly shit.

Backing away. "Sorry." Hand up in a kind of wave. "I am really sorry," turning, "Sorry." I head away from the lady, toward the front of the store, drop the basket at the door and head out to the safety of the car. I'm going to get the chili stuff at the other store across town.

July 15, 2014, 1:43 a.m.

Dear Steve,

What the hell was that, man? Hey, we all make mistakes. It's OK. Nobody got hurt, just a shot to your pride there, right? Awkward but not too bad. Do you know what your mistake was? As a person with a disability, you need to have open, clear communication about your disability. Most times you do, I know that. But sometimes you're taken off guard and you're a little less confident, and you falter. I know there are physical changes with your symptoms, even daily changes, but this is your problem and you need to figure some way through it. And you will. Recognize your mistakes and work on changing them, OK? Here are a few things you might want to think on a bit. Have you fully accepted yourself? You should look into that. What does the man in the glass think about this? What is the quiet *hey* voice telling you? What did your dad tell you?

Sending you a "bro hug,"
Steve

Bang Bang Tap Tap

When Tracey and I had our first child, we had a few discussions about what we would do for communication systems. We went ahead with the sign language preschool, and that went OK for a while. One of the issues that came up was when she would be out of the house and I would be alone with the little one — eventually ones. First I used the light that flashes when the baby cries or makes noise. So imagine doing something like cooking or dishes, and every time the baby moves, it flashes. Then you're unsure if it's a crying flash or just a moving-around flash, so you go check. Eventually you're just checking every 20 seconds. But I suspect all new parents do this anyway. So when they got older, I trained them to bang on the wall next to the crib. I could usually hear or feel the low vibrations. So they started banging to get my attention. This carried on until present times, about 12 years now. They have been banging for 12 fucking years! And not just banging — they took to tapping me whenever they say anything to make sure I'm looking at them.

Tap-tap. "Dad?" (It's my daughter.)

Tap-tap/pull shirt. "You know ick ure eyeade yez tur — ay?"

"What?"

Tap. "You know that picture I made yesterday?" Yelling just below maximum volume.

"Ummmm, yeah?"

Tap. "Air-u Puddit?"

"Your picture of the pudding? Please use your hands! Sign!"

Tap-tap. "Where did you put the picture?" This time with sign support on "where-you-place picture."

So there is quite a lot of banging on the walls, tables and couches, and tapping of my body, mostly my arms and legs, or whatever is closest to their hands. It works so well at getting my attention that my wife does it now too. Sometimes we think the cat understands that she needs to physically touch me to get my attention. I have no one to blame for this but myself. I taught them to do it, and I made them do it. But damn, is it getting irritating.

March 2, 2014, 2:16 a.m.

Dear Steve,

Stevie! Stay positive. Sure, that could get irritating, but you have a beautiful, supportive family that is working with you and trying hard to communicate with you. Remember what your friend who was battling cancer told you when you asked him for advice. He said, "If you're feeling lousy, and if you're suffering, try to keep things as normal as you can. Don't take it out on others. Especially your family. Keep it normal, and normal will start to feel normal again."

Your friend,
Steve

Quin-Oh'Ah

As a Deaf adult, I've repeatedly found myself in situations where I have to speak a word I've never heard before. I was taking a class on philosophies of education, and we studied the writings of Piaget (Pee-ah-jay), a founder of constructivist methods in education. The entire semester I was reading along or watching the interpreter spell the name Piaget. At the end of the class, I presented my project with visuals and a speech in which I referred to Piaget as "Pie-get" about 15 times. At the end of the presentation, the teacher pointed out the correct pronunciation, to which I regrettably exclaimed to the class, "No fuckin' way!" We all laughed, and this awesome teacher then pointed out that this was the perfect example of Piaget's teachings. Our exposure to something new, our misconceptions, the "Aha!" moment and then the understanding comprise the flowchart of true learning, according to Piaget.

One evening, Tracey and I were getting ready to go to a potluck dinner. "What are you making for the party?" she asks. "We should probably bring a salad; they always have a bunch of Costco appetizers there. A salad would be a good addition."

My wife does not cook much. She says Italians have the reins in the kitchen, and as our years together accumulated, she slowly but consistently withdrew from cooking. I don't mind much. When I'm alone in the kitchen, I find it to be a peaceful and creative place. A welcomed, silent communication between me and the food, the knife, the heat and the spice. A distraction from the tinnitus noises and strain of communicating with hearing people. When others are in the kitchen, I often find it hard to stay. They are noisily clanking, clanging, banging and crashing the pots, pans, plates, mugs and silverware. These sounds are my kryptonite, my nemesis. My hyperacusis nemesis.

"I'm going to make the quin-oh'ah with the black beans," I say. Southwestern style, some red onion, chipotle spices."

She looks at me a little strangely but says, "OK, great!"
At the party that night, I proudly announce that we brought "a southwestern quin-oh'ah" for the potluck—to which the host replies, "Huh? What's that?" Then looking in the bowl, she says, "Oh! Quinoa! Great, thanks. You know that grain is pronounced *keen-wa*?"

To which I regrettably reply, "No fuckin' way!" Then, "Hey Honey! This stuff is called *keen-wa*. Did you know that?"

"Yeah," she says.

"So, uh ... how come you never told me? Or even today, in the kitchen, when I told you what I was going to make for tonight? You didn't say anything."

"Well, I didn't really understand what you were talking about then but just trusted that you were going to make something good," she states with a big, toothy, brownnosing smile.

June 12, 2014, 3:12 a.m.

Dear Steve,

Nobody is passing judgment on you because of your deafness.
Stop judging yourself.

Love,
Steve

The Cochlear Implant Decision

<u>I'm not ready</u>

Tracey and I threw around the implant idea a bunch, but I was reluctant to take a chance on a change in my residual hearing situation because I was still able to write and record music with the 15-ish percent residual hearing that I had. Over the years, I had developed a system to adapt to the gradual loss of hearing with several accommodations. These systems allowed me to continue to express myself with music and participate socially and professionally in the music community.

Music adaptations were a combination of clever use of technology and mental and physical training. I would use devices such as amplification, tonal effects or even visual cues such as watching the recorded session on digital linear graphing software — which is how all digital recording software is now. You can pretty much watch the notes coming at you like that video game Guitar Hero. While writing, I often used a device called an octaver, which transfers notes played to different octaves — in my case, lower and lower down into the lowest bass register I could get. So a screeching high E played on the 12th fret on the guitar could be sent through this device and it would sound like a low E — two to three octaves lower.

The 15-ish percent hearing I had was all around and below the 500 Hz range, which is like the left eighth of a grand piano being played across the street and down the block. So I could write melody lines in their proper position and "hear" them a few octaves lower to be able to check and work them, harmonize them and build chords around them. I could basically still write the ideas I had in my head and almost hear them (octavized) to be able to check them. I could still write songs with chord progressions, melodies and harmonies. I would need to practice over and over and train my head to "hear" the song when it's played, even though I can't actually hear it. Embed it in my brain and make it like a muscle memory.

Next I would do basic recordings of the sections in their "real tone range" to share with the other players. Then we would all get together and I could double-check the writing through the practice sessions before recording. I recorded about a dozen full records like this.

Another adaptation for my music playing was developing systems of communication with the players. I continued to work with my old friend Mark. Over the years, we played hundreds of shows and made a dozen or so records. My hearing kept declining, and we kept evolving our music communication system. Signals, signs and visual cues. Redundancy of rehearsal to the point at which each of us knows what the other guy is going to do before he does it. If one of us had the slightest misstep in timing or note, the other would give a little raised-eyebrow glance within a half of a second to make sure all is OK and kind of say "Dude, WTF?" It was quite a system, and I've been lucky to mesh chemically and musically with a great friend.

We both ended up living in the same town and still continue to write, play, record and perform. My music projects slowed down as we all started families and held down day jobs, but it was still a very important part of my life that single-handedly held me back from the assumed benefits of the cochlear implant.

How much worse can it get?

In our house, we use a system of sign-supported speech or whatever we can to get the information out. A combination of signing, speaking, yelling, writing and acting things out. Call it a "total communication" type of system.

My hearing declined over the years to the point at which Tracey and I couldn't converse while sitting on the couch in a quiet house. As new parents of elementary school students, we would need to have meetings on the "meeting couch." The so-called meetings weren't much more than a 30-second blur of logistical information being forced out in frustration because of the anticipated interruption from the kids coming downstairs and jumping and jabbering at us.

We would realize some changes in my hearing through these conversations. "So, honey, last week, I was hearing better, no?" Or "I can't understand you right now, honey. Too much, too fast, and I think last month I was getting it all on the first or second run-through. Ugh!"

The meetings weren't the best situations for a Deaf person, but after years of consistently having them in the same spot, with the same background noise, it became a good assessment tool. Usually Tracey would start, and I would ask questions about things I missed.

"OK, so, tomorrow morning I have an early meeting. Amma will go to Kate's, and she will bring her to school. I will drop Albert off early, and then you have that quickie meeting after school and then that doctor's appointment. Albert needs to go to intramural football. After the doctor, you pick up Amma and bring her to dance class, but pick her up early, at 6 instead of 6:30, to get her over to the soccer practice so she can get in on the team pictures. Bring her good uniform. Leave the key out back for Albert to get in the house after football. Make sure Albert does Part 1 and 2 for the science fair project—due Wednesday! And when they step into the house, make sure they take off all their dance and sports stuff and bag it so I know where it is for next time. I'm sick of looking for their shit two minutes before we're supposed to get across town for their activities. And I guess you better pick up Chipotle burritos or something kind of healthy. I'm going on a hike with Mary tomorrow because it's Mom Night. Is that cool? Can I meet up with Mary tomorrow?"

Thirty seconds of hell for a Deaf lip-reader, and that's just Monday's meeting. Every day's preparation for the next day seems like a CIA mission.

You're Deaf

Oct 3, 2013, 7:42 am. Basement bathroom.
"You're Deaf," I tell the man in the glass.

October 4, 2013, 12:32 a.m.

Dear Steve,

This is it, huh? You're finally there? You can't hear the music anymore? You can't hear your daughter's voice? You're not communicating with hearing people anymore? "A baby's cry, a woman's sigh, a child's why, the long goodbye." You wrote those lyrics when you were 17. You're ready, man. You're doing well. Acceptance is the only way on this one. You've been preparing yourself for this since you were 12, Steve. Remember all those self-tests you gave yourself each morning by tapping the various things near your bed to see what you could hear that day? You're ready for this. You've been getting ready for this day for, well, it seems like forever. I'm sorry, but I'm glad you're facing it now, head-on. Accepting it. It's a bitter pill, buddy. Come here. Come here, man.

A full-body hug,

Love,
Steve

The Implant

Ready

Communication with hearing people in the manner in which I'd communicated for the past 30 years was becoming impossible as my hearing declined, and I decided to begin the steps necessary to finally get the implant. Communication had been pretty bad these past few years, and it was getting even worse. The implant was helping many people — it could only help us, right?

I knew the implant was not something that would help my music recognition. We were hoping it would improve my voice recognition. At first I tried to convince myself that I would again be able to devise a system to "hear" and play music with the new stimulus from the implant, but I was beginning to accept that music might not work out after the implant surgery. I knew I'd have to work through that loss further, but enhancing communication with humanity seemed like a good tradeoff. Mark and I did some work on a bunch of songs I had in the vault, and we finished up a really great recording — something that I was comfortable with possibly being my last.

I started seeing the audiologist and went through all the prescreening for the implant. Everything was in order for surgery, and I seemed to be a really good candidate because I had a solid background of sound and language from birth through my early teens. However, there was some concern about the implanted ear not having been stimulated for so long because I never wore hearing aids. The doctor warned me that it would probably be a long assimilation period for my brain after activation. We set up the surgery for midwinter, a slow season for Tracey and I at work.

About a month before the surgery, I freaked out and decided to go to the studio and do some recording. I felt like I needed to get some ideas recorded — ideas that had been building up over the years as I watched the kids grow through elementary school. A bunch of melodies, chants and lullabies that Tracey and I would make up over the years with them. When we put the ideas together, we realized we had a solid collection of children's songs, enough for a complete project. I got some players together and we recorded the foundation tracks for the album. We laid down tracks for drums, upright bass, tuba and guitar. The foundations of the songs were digitally recorded, cleaned up and ready for any future accompaniments. I had written out and recorded melodies for the accompanying instruments and vocals that I would complete sometime in the future when the implant issues stabilized. I was feeling better now, more content and ready for the transition.

Surgery

My surgery went well, but I had a rough few weeks afterward with the recovery medications. On the third night after surgery, I woke up in the middle of the night and stumbled toward the shifting blue-green shadows from the night-light in the bathroom of my basement. I lifted the lid, let out a little sigh, started the stream, and *holy shit! I can hear my pee!* I was in a bit of shock, trying to keep it centered. What the hell? Can the implant be stimulating my cochlea through vibrations or something even though it hasn't been activated yet? I finished up and closed the door and *squeak!* — the door hinge. I was hearing things I hadn't heard in a long, long time that week. Computer start-up beeps, my son's violin and melodies of old songs I knew.

After talking to the doctors and doing some tests, we figured out that the steroid drug, Prednisone, was responsible for the increase in hearing. The surgeon had put me on the medication in efforts to protect my residual hearing after the surgery. It's also used for patients who have sudden deafness. While on the drug, my hearing increased 15 dB—the equivalent of doubling my hearing. It was a very interesting week of remembering old sounds with my natural hearing, and it brought up some thoughts that there might be some available hearing in there. Why is it suppressed, and how can we retrieve it?

After stopping the steroids, my hearing declined again to the pre-surgery levels—back to the 15 percent hearing that I was living with for a decade or two. After much consultation with doctors of all sorts, we concluded that the area is regularly inflamed, and only the strength of the Prednisone could reduce that. We have not been able to replicate that period of clarity and residual hearing increase through other means of inflammation reduction such as those related to diet, allergy or the environment.

181

Activation

"*Holy shit!*" I whisper to the audiologist. "*Turn it down! Down* ....
way down." I can't even raise my voice above a whisper. Barely even
whispering now, just mouthing, "*Down!*" My wife and I are at the
audiologist's office for the initial activation of the implant.

"IT'S ALL THE WAY DOWN." She's smiling, kind of
apprehensively, because, from her experience with all her
patients, she knows this is an overwhelming transition, but she
can't ever really experience it, so she just keeps saying, "YOUR
BRAIN WILL ADJUST. EVERYONE FEELS LIKE THIS." It sounds
like she is inside my head, talking to me through a megaphone.
Echoes and squeaks galore.

"*Please turn it down....*" whispering.

For about a week or two, the implant produced all space sounds
and whistles and zeeepies, shweeeepies and zuurps. Voices, as I
tried to lip-read them, were robotic and tinny. This was not what
I was hoping for. I was hoping for some control. To be able to
slowly turn up the volume and slowly work it in. A little bit each
day? When I feel comfortable at one level, I'll boost it a bit.

I figured out it doesn't work like that. The implant pretty much
needs to be ON and needs to stay ON. Sleep with it ON if you can,
they said. "Put it as high as you can deal with and leave it on as
much as you can," said the audiologist and every other person in
the Department of Hearing Sciences. "The more you have it on,
the quicker your brain will adjust."

So I'm trying really hard to do just that and totally freaking out.
Really losing my crapola. I know I've been cursing a lot, but I need
one right here, in capital letters; there is no other adjective to do
this feeling justice — everything seems REALLY FUCKING LOUD!
Loud, as if I were in the street and a muffler-less motorcycle gang
came by, shooting off mortars, throwing grenades, blowing air
horns and making this type of REALLY FUCKING LOUD sound,
and I would cry, puke, shit my pants, fall on the ground and bleed

out of my ears. I was feeling like this for a few weeks while trying to go to work and do other crazy things, like talk to people. I was told to try to block out the crap and focus on what the real sounds are, and the brain would put it together. The weird space sounds will go away and things will start to make more sense, they said.

Back when the doctors expressed concern about the fact that I hadn't been stimulating that area of the cochlea for so long, this effect was the reason. It's a major shock to the system. Patients who wore hearing aids seem to have an easier time with the activation, but I never wore them. I have the type of residual hearing that can't really be amplified. To do so, it would have had to be jacked up to over 100 dB — almost the level of a jet engine and just brutally painful to people that have hyperacusis.

WHAM!

Science can seem like magic if you don't understand the science of it. Magic is actually a lot of science. I understand the science behind the implant, and it still seems like magic. Basically a flick of a switch and my hearing in the right ear goes from 0 to 80 dB, at 22 points or tone clusters in the cochlear, in a half second. WHAM!

Breathing, cloth brushing against cloth, people moving, walking, shoes sliding, the fridge humming, the heater fan and the flames themselves, the cat claws on the floor, water running somewhere through pipes, a couple of computer fans?—holy shit!—people talking everywhere, and the kids are really loud! *Oh my God, do we always let them act like this?* The goddamn papers ruffling? Plates and forks and spoons, and the PLASTIC BAGS! HOLY SHIT! All the plastic bag-type shit is the noisiest of all! When my wife is taking something out of a plastic supermarket sack on the other side of the kitchen, it sounds to me like there is a little munchkin guy standing on my earlobe, crumpling up those crispy-type plastic candy bags through a mini-munchkin megaphone set on volume 12. How do hearing people do it? I can't even hold a complete thought like this. I step back for a bit and watch the commotion in the kitchen and living room and remember that I trained my kids to bang on walls and tap me to get my attention and then to talk really loudly. Damn.

I really tried hard to work it those first few weeks, and it did start to go the way they said it would. We managed to almost clear out the whistles and space sounds, and I was beginning to isolate voices. They were still robotic, but they were starting to change. There are programs to work through, training the brain to the new sounds, and I was working the programs very diligently. Just having the implant activated and doing normal daily activities was exhausting in the sense of mental fatigue because my brain was working overtime to try to process all the new stimuli.

March 11, 2014, 2:02 a.m.

Dear Steve,

Weird, overwhelming and at times unbearable, but a MIRACLE is what it is. Be grateful that something like this is even available for you, Steve. You should have a deep appreciation for this opportunity. Deep gratitude for science, scientists, doctors, researchers and all related professionals who have worked to develop medicine to this extent.

With much appreciation,
Steven L. DiCesare

The Good, the Bad and the Haze

Over the next month after the surgery, patterns started to form. There were a bunch of good days and a bunch of bad days. Good days were approaching the point where I wasn't thinking about the new sounds and being stimulated and distracted by them every second of the whole day. So maybe half of all the seconds in the day, I could concentrate on other thoughts. I was pretty happy about this and thinking positively about the future of the device. I figured it would just keep getting better and I'd regain my pre-surgery peace of mind and clearheaded freedom of thought.

Then there were the bad days. The sound stimuli I received through the implant would change from a comfortable level to a more severe intensity, triggering my hyperacusis. I would be cringing, backing away from loud scenes, hiding in the basement, getting irritated with everyone, feeling frustrated with the device and basically freaking out all day. Most times it would just be the way I woke up, and things would stay at that level throughout the day. Sometimes the change would happen suddenly for no apparent reason. One time I went for a short jog, and afterward it jacked up into the bad zone. Another time I was sitting on the couch after the kids were in bed, and suddenly it jacked into the bad zone. I could suddenly hear Tracey clicking away on the laptop in the other room, the dishwasher became a raging mechanical monster, and the heater fan would sound like a jet plane. This is not a dramatization. My perception of the sounds around me would change in this manner in an instant.

I kept journals and logs and studied the patterns, trying to determine the cause for these changes over the next few weeks while trying to "keep it on." "Keep it running" and "Power through," as the doctors kept saying. What was the cause of these changes? Was it the device? Was it my body chemistry? Was it the implant stimuli whacking my brain out? Maybe the stimulation

189

was just too much, and my brain tweaks out after a while on it? We did thorough checks on the device and virtually eliminated the possibility of a faulty processor or faulty mechanics.

I've always had fluctuating symptoms with my hearing. Some days might be bad because of weather conditions, fatigue or inflammation, or environmental or chemical influences. Some days the tinnitus would be louder or softer, but as far as I can remember, it was always the same kind of sound: a high-pitched ringing or hissing. We started to look more in depth into how the chemical fluctuations in my body might be affecting my response to the implant stimulus. Is my changing sensitivity issue causing me to perceive that the implant levels are changing?

For example, let's suppose I had a couple beers last night and slept poorly while a low-pressure storm system blew in. Pre-surgery, with this situation, I might have a few days of "bad hearing" that would drop me into a funky type of "poopy head" haze. I'd be feeling kind of dopey, foggy and slow-thinking. Communication would be way down, and I would need multiple repeats with sign support. When I'm in the poopy-head haze, I don't put effort forth to communicate, which makes it even worse. Was the poopy-head haze altering my perception of the implant stimuli post-surgery?

Wuss!

I just read about a 9-year-old who is losing his eyesight. He will be blind by the time he is 10 or 11.

I recently saw a guy in my son's school in a wheelchair, with a rod attached to his head that I figured to be for communicating.

My neighbor across the street has been waiting for a heart transplant for almost six years now. He carries around these pumps and tanks and all kinds of gear. All day and night.

Why am I being such a wuss? Why am I even wasting my time at 3 a.m. writing this stuff down? I could be working on lessons for class or doing something for my kids and family or making art or doing something worthwhile for the house or community.

May 18, 2014, 3:07 a.m.

Dear Steve,

Dude, again, this is your problem, not someone else's. Own it. Don't judge or compare yourself with others. Not your distresses or your successes. Follow your own path and judge yourself on your own accomplishments and failures.

And you decided to write this stuff down to share with people like you who are going through a lot of the same stuff you did. Remember? They might not have any support, or answers to questions, and they will appreciate your experiences and humor. Keep going, and stop complaining.

Best,
Steve

The Flood

We started to look at how the fluctuations within my body could be affecting my response to the implant stimulus. We saw the doctors again, and they wanted me to try a medicine that some people with Meniere's disease have had some success with. *Meniere's disease? No way! I have Meniere's disease?* A lot of my symptoms with my hearing loss, fluctuations, dizzy poopy-head haze and tinnitus led the doctors to state I probably have something similar to Meniere's disease, if not the actual disease. *What the hell is Meniere's disease?* They can't really do a thorough diagnosis on it because of my severe-to-profound hearing loss. Evidently, you need to have a good bit of hearing to be able to test for Meniere's, and it doesn't really matter if you have a true diagnosis or not because the treatments are the same anyway: diuretics with some dietary and nutrient support. I was kind of psyched! *Finally some answers. I have Meniere's disease (maybe).* So I'm going deaf and I have Meniere's disease to maybe explain these weird fluctuations with the tinnitus and the dizzy poopy-haze stuff. *All right!*

Over the next few weeks, I started to take the implant off when it jacked into the bad zone, and then I would try it again the next morning to see if I could deal. On and off, off and on, contradictory to what the doctors were telling me to do. I could pretty much tell if it was going to be a good day or bad day without the implant on just by the type of hearing, tinnitus or poopy head I was having that morning when I woke up. So, I was very excited to try the diuretics and decided to assess their results without the implant on. I wanted to test and see what the medicine could do to the symptoms without the added stimuli and distraction from the implant.

I started the diuretic drugs and left the implant off. Strange things started happening within the first few days. I would get weird types of side effects — vomiting and strange aches in my back and thighs. We figured out that I had to make sure I took the medicine after a very big meal. We got that figured out, and a few days later, a bunch of other stuff began. The "tinnitus flood" introduced itself to me one night by way of a group of angels.

I awoke to a choir of what sounded like angel voices repeating a phrase from what seemed like a verse from Come Sail Away by Styx. It was spacy, sustained and sounded like a synthesizer set on the "angel choir" program. I couldn't understand the words, and it was sort of just the melody of the singing, but harmonized. It was definitely in my head, and I couldn't seem to stop it from sequencing over and over. This was the start of the flood.

My lifelong tinnitus noise is a high-pitched ringing or hissing sound in both ears fluctuating around a level of 3 out of $10-10$ being bad. So, imagine that 30 percent of what you hear is a high-pitched ringing or hissing. In the first few days of taking the medication sans implant, I started having a bunch of new tinnitus noises that built up and out and around and basically just took over my life ... and these continued for a year and a half. The tinnitus flood.

The first of the flood was the angel voices, which I call Radio Broadcast. Sometimes there are musical angel-choir-type sequences and sometimes voices, like a radio broadcast from the 50s-style radio. This seems to always be a male-sounding voice with clear and distinct diction but indecipherable words. It's like the parents' voices on the old Charlie Brown cartoons. In other versions of this, I hear a chorus of angel voices repeating musical phrases over and over, like I had that first night. I hear them in harmony, two and sometimes three voices if I concentrate. I later found out that other people have this, and it is a diagnosed condition called nonpsychotic auditory hallucination syndrome. *Whew! Hell yeah!*

The second part of the tinnitus flood is what I call Wind Through the Cave in a Storm. It's like a howling wind sound or a washout wave rolling in and out of my head through both ears. This one is a little scary because it can get pretty fierce. Fierce as in visions of a tsunami washing over a city block. Fierce like the stormy midnight waves crashing against the lighthouse out there all alone in the middle of the harbor. Fierce like you should sit down right this second or hold onto the wall.

The third I call Trains-Come-a-Roaring. This is either a clicking or a rhythmic tone that sounds like an engine. Fast and repetitive rotations that my musical mind would label as something like a 16th note, or a whole bunch of hits per second. The sound of a train running over a rickety section of tracks kind of nails it. I believe this to be some sort of "hearing" of bodily functions — like blood running through valves near my ear.

The last of the tinnitus flood is what I call the Coach's Whistle. This is a positional noise when I tilt my head to the right side. This is the most distinct as well as the clearest and loudest of the whole flood. Unlike the others, it has an on/off switch. I move to that position and the whistle blows steady and clear until I move back.

Additionally, my lifelong tinnitus hissing jacks up to 5ish out of 10. All the tinnitus flood sounds fluctuate as well. Some days they're on the right side, one or two of them on the left, sometimes both sides, all of them changing levels, and coming and going.

All this came on during a three-week period. I began waking up after a few hours of sleep in a state of emotion that I have never really felt before: despair.

The doctors tell me to expect some changes. The medicines could whack you out a bit, but you need to "power through" for 30 days. The meds should calm you down, and the flood should go away as your body balances out. Then we can get the implant on again, which will most likely compress the tinnitus noises, and the brain will begin to eliminate them or block them out.

197

I powered through for a bit. But the tinnitus flood kept raging. So I stopped the meds short of a month. It was a bad year. Tracey says she secretly had me on suicide watch. Spring to summer into fall, trying to get a handle on why this happened. Trying to reverse it. Trying to deal with it. I saw more than 24 different doctors and practitioners of alternative medicine over the next year. Despair.

September 2, 2014, 1:51 a.m.

Dear Steve,

Hang in there, man! Keep trying and don't give up. You will figure this out. You will get through this. Let's think back to something terrible that happened to you ... the worst thing that happened to you in your life. Not when you got dumped by your first girlfriend—worse. Not when they didn't let you into the graduate program because your grades were poor and you had to do an extra year of classes—worse. Not being the only Deaf person at your job, in your social circle and in your community—worse. Not the whole 30 years of gradually losing your hearing—worse. Remember those last couple of weeks before your dad passed away from cancer. Remember one of the last things he said to you? When he saw you in despair at his suffering? He said, "Hey Steve, we are going to get through this. Stata-ten, you understand?"

Hang in there.

Love,
Steve

25 Doctors

Over the next year, I saw a heck of a lot of doctors. I've lost count, but I visited somewhere around 25 different doctors/healers in efforts to gain an understanding about the tinnitus flood and possibly reverse it. I hadn't seen a doctor in about 15 years before that — other than my primary care physician and the cochlear implant personnel — and after 25 different doctors, with multiple visits, I'm still suffering from the same symptoms I've had most of my life, plus the tinnitus flood.

Now I know there are people out there who are really suffering. I mean, I don't even have real physical pain or anything like that related to the deafness. I realize how lucky I am. I've seen others suffering. But I forget that so quickly on those days that the tinnitus flood is raging. The trains are running through my head, the whistles blowing when I tilt my head to the right, the waves crashing, motors running, the bleeps and buzzes. The inability to complete a sentence through all the distractions. This past year, I realize now that I've been alternating between hiding in my basement and coming upstairs and yelling at everyone, angry and irritated and just trudging through the day.

"You should put the implant back on and try these antidepressants and power through. These should mellow you out a little bit and maybe calm the nerves in your head," says the MD.

"Let's try these herbal drops. This one, this one and this one in the morning and night. This in the morning only, and this one before bed. Stay on the anti-inflammation diet for 40 days and let's see if we can reduce inflammation in there. Do not cheat at all with the diet. Maybe you have an allergy to a food that's causing inflammation and irritating your tinnitus," says the naturopath.

"Seems like your hips are misaligned, which might be causing tension in your spine and neck area. That could be causing the whistle tinnitus and others. Let's work through some adjustments," says the chiropractor.

"You have a twisted group of muscles in your neck here that could be sending inappropriate signals to your ear mechanisms, like a misfiring situation. We need to sort this out," says the physical therapist.

"I feel that this might be stemming from the kidneys. I think there is a kidney yin deficiency. There is probably some nerve miscommunication going on, and we could work on inflammation and overall body health," says the acupuncturist.

"No, not everybody's neck and shoulders feel sore all the time. Yours are hurting my hands. It feels like I'm massaging a tree trunk. We need to loosen things up here. This tension could be escalating your symptoms," says the massage therapist.

"Your jaw is misaligned, and you have some TMJ going on. This could be a cause of your tinnitus. We could adjust your bite for sure and hope that it helps your symptoms. It might, it might not," says the neuromuscular dental professional.

"You're allergic to pollen, mostly … and dog and cat dander, but I don't think these allergies are causing your tinnitus symptoms," says the allergist.

"You should tell Tracey that more sex is the only thing that helps your symptoms," says my buddy Mark.

August 24, 2014, 1:54 a.m.

Dear Steve,

Listen to Mark.

From
Steve

Implant! Me — No!

After taking our order and giving me a receipt, the cashier at Chick-fil-A waves me to follow her as she comes around the counter and ushers me and my kids across the restaurant dining area. She is talking to my son, and he keeps turning around to look at me. I have no idea what's going on.

Holding my daughter's hand and following my son and the cashier, I'm confused as she leads us across the restaurant. My son keeps glancing at me, and he's doing the questioning-eyes thing he does to me when he is getting anxious. We arrive at a table where a couple is eating, and the cashier asks my son something I don't understand. My son nods, turns to the diners, and signs and speaks, "All OK (thumbs-up), you need more?" They shake their head and sign back, "Thumbs-up, thanks." Now I'm understanding. *Signing people! Yeah!*

The cashier should have just written to the diners, but whatever. Unaware of how her action might isolate any number of either of our groups, she was just trying to be friendly and helpful.

I introduce myself and send the kids to a table. One of the first questions asked of me whenever I meet Deaf people is whether I am hearing or Deaf. Just about every time. Sometimes even before asking my name. It's a basis for connection in the Deaf community. For instance, hearing people might ask, "Where are you from? Where did you grow up?" In much the same way, asking your hearing status gives Deaf people something to relate to and a basis for conversation. If you are Deaf, we might have had the same experiences, spent time at the same or similar school, or taken the same class. If you are hard of hearing, we might have known the same people or visited the same audiologist.

I tell the diners I am late-Deaf, meaning I came to ASL and Deaf culture late in life. Therefore, ASL wouldn't be my first language, and Deaf culture was not the culture I was raised in.

Although the question is usually "Deaf or hearing," I sometimes feel that the underlying question is really *Deaf* or *deaf*. The difference is the affiliation to Deaf culture in contrast to being physically deaf and not a participant in the Deaf community or a user of ASL. After talking to this couple for a few minutes, I realized this was their question. They wanted to know if I was "big D" Deaf or "little d" deaf, and they seemed to make the assumption that I was little "d" deaf when they noticed my cochlear implant. When I identified myself as Deaf, part of the Deaf community and a Deaf Education teacher, the woman just blew me off and ignored me after signing, "Implant! Me — NO! Not interested." She went back to eating a chicken sandwich and didn't make eye contact with me for the remainder of the three-minute conversation.

The rest of the conversation was a series of attack questions from the man — very personal and offensive questions into my life and my decision to get implanted. After three minutes of defending myself, I realized how inappropriate it was for this conversation to be happening — in this place and at the onset of a first meeting. I was a bit upset. I excused myself from the man in midsentence and actually tapped the woman's shoulder across the table so she had to look at me. I signed, "Nice to meet you, enjoy your night" and headed over to meet up with my kids for a chicken nugget fest.

July 12, 2014, 2:36 a.m.

Dear Steve,

You know what happened here. It's happened before. You've been through it. We've all been through it. You let them open up that little bag of self-doubt we all carry around in our baggage. You let them pull the old "You're not cool enough for the cool group" thing on you. In this case, You're not Deaf enough. *You grew up hearing; then you went ahead and got a cochlear implant. You're a robot now. You're not proud of your birth self.*

Remember, Steve, every culture has this issue, but let me tell you again. You're Deaf enough. There are all different kinds of Deaf. There's the big "D," the little "d," and lots of different fonts and sizes in between. You know this. Well-educated and accustomed to the many different views in the Deaf community, you know some people feel very strongly about their cultural well-being and are protective of it. Remember that the encounter in Chick-fil-A is an anomaly for you. Your usual encounters, through your travels, with random Deaf people, deaf people, hard-of-hearing people and signers are usually exciting and memorable. Yeah! A signer! Someone like you, or kind of like you, or at least they probably know someone like you. You will have a lot in common, lots of things to connect on, plenty to talk about and plenty to laugh about. Remember that you always look forward to meeting other Deaf people, deaf people and hard-of-hearing people, and you're always on the lookout for signing people in your travels. You're Deaf enough, Steve.

Keep looking!
Steve

Eye Contact

I approach the check-in desk and give the receptionist my name and the name of the doctor I'm supposed to be seeing today. The secretary says something to me, but she is looking down and sideways at her files and clipboards. "Humbl- quazi nehunder garble-shander, and franzi- kidles ack-oopere," she says as she hands me a clipboard with a bunch of papers that I assume are the regular first-visit check-in papers. After this year and all the doctor visits, I cruise through these papers in under three minutes. Patient history, reason for visit, current medications and so on. There are four other people in the waiting room; two were filling out the forms when I got there and they are still filling them in. I'm rocking today, I totally blew them away.

I congratulate myself as I march back up to the receptionist desk and edge the clipboard over the rim of the counter to spark her attention. She is on the phone and typing on the computer, but she sees me and takes my clipboard. I'm about to turn away when I remember that I better tell her I'm Deaf and to write a note on top of my form there — that "patient is Deaf." I hang there for a bit, waiting for her to get off the phone. After a few minutes she does and says, "Ake ase — t, and d — ursl wil cum — — lu oona," with a hand pointing over to the seats. I figure she is telling me to take a seat, and they will call me. The usual system. I say "OK, thanks. I am Deaf and I am thinking you should probably write that on the top of the form because I miss a lot of nurses' announcements when they call my name. The nurse can wave, throw something, use spitballs, kick me, shoot me with a Nerf gun, boomerang a tongue depressor, slingshot some Q-tips at me, or whatever she wants. Thanks!"

Many times I sit through the "Steve. Steve DiCesare. Steve?" announcement because I get caught up in the front sections of Us Weekly and People Magazine, where all the celebrities are walking their dogs in their thongs and bikinis. I miss the announcement, the staff gets confused, and they pass on me and take the next few patients. Eventually I get frustrated and check in with them. The receptionist either realizes she forgot to write the Deaf notice on top of my form, or she actually did and then she goes to talk to the nurse on the side, where they look at my form together and then point at me and nod. I wave back and smile and sit down again with the celebrities who are "Just Like Us."

Just a few weeks ago I went to get a haircut at Sport Clips. I checked in by giving my phone number and asked the girl to please note "Deaf guy, tall, dark, handsome, blue shirt" on the receipt for the stylists. It was a busy place, and there were lots of magazines and TVs with sports games on them, but I was feeling confident that this time, it was going to work out. I settled in with some magazines and sports and was sure they would come and get me. I wasn't counting the people in front of me, just relaxing and confident I nailed it this time. But 40 minutes later, I went up to check, and the receptionist floundered for my receipt and said, "Oh, we called you a while ago, did you step out?"

But on this occasion, in the doctor's office, I did what I needed to do with the receptionist, advocating for my needs, and I turn around and scan for the right seat. Looking for something in the corner, facing outward in case ninjas attack, but also near the magazines pile, but not right on top of it. I don't want to have to make people climb over me every time they want a new magazine. I also don't really want to be sitting next to anyone if I can help it. You know, with the germs and all that business. So in that one-second frame of time, I analyze the situation and decide to grab a magazine and head over to the far wall, focusing on germ clearance rather than magazine proximity.

The nurse opens the entrance door and calls out a name. There are five people in here—one person still on the forms—so it's a 25 percent chance that it's me. She's looking around, curious, and about to repeat the name when the old guy on the right-hand wall starts to get up. *Whew, it's him.* I start getting into the magazine, and with the bikini shots, start to fade out of the waiting room, onto the beach. BAM! The nurse, not in a bikini, is standing in front of me, with a form, saying "Eve, Eye says Sare?"

"What? Sorry, I'm Deaf. I'm Steve."

She looks at the form again and says, "Yes, Steve, Di-Says-Sare?"

"Oh yeah, that's me." Thrown off by the mispronunciation of my last name.

We go through the door and corridors and arrive in one of the patient visiting rooms. The nurse motions for me to sit on the patient exam table. I usually sit upright on here and check out the posters of ears and throats while waiting. The nurse does the blood pressure tests, gives me the thumbs-up and excuses herself. A short time later, the door opens and the doctor comes in. A 40-something blonde woman wearing nice professional-type street clothes. A professional doctor-type skirt and a button-up shirt, with a button-up sweater that is left open and hanging at her sides. She introduces herself and asks what I came in for today. I introduce myself and let her know that I am Deaf and read lips. I do fairly well lip-reading with doctor visits in a one-on-one situation in a quiet room.

She takes a seat on the small roller stool that the doctors usually sit on, and I stay sitting on the high exam table. We start to discuss the reason for the visit and she types a bunch on the laptop sitting on her lap, taking notes, I assume. Then asks some questions and closes her sweater, very tightly, covering her breasts. After all my years and all my experiences, I know this signal; this happens a lot with me. We discuss more, she types, her sweater opens a bit again, and she lifts her head up to ask some more questions and closes her sweater again. Not in an insulting way. I can tell she doesn't even realize she is doing it. She is getting very into my story and diagnosing my problem. We discuss more, she types and her sweater opens a bit again, then she raises her head and we talk more while she closes her sweater again. She is not realizing it; it's obviously just a knee-jerk reaction for her. She types some more, the sweater opens, and then she lifts her head and talks more as she closes her sweater again.

I am really making an effort to not look down her shirt, alternating between focusing on her lips and quick flashes on her eyes. Commonly when I lip-read women who are not familiar with people who read lips, my eye contact with their lips is interpreted as "He's not looking at my eyes, he's looking further down, he's looking at my breasts." This situation was made a bit worse because of the seating arrangement.

Should I tell her to relax? "I am not looking at your breasts"? No. Bad idea. She doesn't even realize she's doing the cover-up thing. She seems pretty comfortable with me otherwise. I could get down and grab that chair in the corner and scoot it over next to her, but that might freak her out. "I am not looking at your breasts, doc, it just seems that way from your angle, when I watch your lips." Nah, I am just going to let it ride. She does the cover-her-breasts thing a few more times during the visit, and I make a mental note to sit in the low chair next time I go to any doctor's office.

June 17, 2014, 3:42 a.m.

Dear Steve,

Yeah man, remember to take the low ground when you can, but stay off your knees. Seriously, isn't that why you have that little spasm in your knees? Fifteen years of teaching and you've been trying to give your students and coworkers the right impression, kneeling in front of their desks. It is what it is. You're Deaf and you read a lot of lips. You met with the man in the glass and you made peace with it. Now you go and make sure you make peace with it in your social community, be up front about it and all will be OK.

From
Steve

Mental Adjustment

It's been a year now since the surgery, and the tinnitus flood is still raging, but I'm starting to figure out how to find some relief by mentally blocking it out. I haven't found any medicine or naturopathic remedies that have helped. In hopes of compressing the flood, I'm planning to reactivate the implant and am feeling pretty positive about the trial. I'm looking forward to sounds again from the implant. And I'm focusing more now on how I react to the symptoms and how I can find a remedy through mental and psychological means. I read somewhere that if you smile and hold it for 20 seconds, you will feel happier, even if you're totally pissed off. Try it, it works. They say if you kiss your spouse for seven seconds every night before bed, you'll feel happier and sleep better. Try it, it works. Will you say the glass is half empty or half full? I'm trying to change the way I look at the symptoms I'm suffering from. A mental adjustment.

When the flood first came and we were looking for some solutions, some relief, my wife once stated, "Captain Kirk (William Shatner) has tinnitus, and he says you need to focus on what you CAN hear." At the time I was thinking, *Fuck Kirk, he obviously isn't dealing with tinnitus at this level, he obviously has some hearing, I can't hear anything BUT this shitstorm in my head.* Recently, with my change in perspective, my mental adjustment, I began to isolate the flood sounds and started to work on mentally blocking them out. I create "rooms" in my head and put each noise in a room and close the door. Of course, at night, when I'm sleeping, the noises sneak out to cause havoc in my dreams, run rampant and have a keg party. I find that early every morning, I need to massage my head and neck and work on breathing and blood flow. I realize this is a form of meditation, and I think this is something you need to come to on your own. Your wife can't force this understanding on you, and neither can Captain Kirk. Similar to the teaching of Piaget, we create our own understanding.

When someone asks what tinnitus noises I have today, I sometimes find myself wondering which. I can go to that room, knock on the door and visit with the noise. It would actually seem to get louder! Then I'd leave the room and close the door again and block it out to some degree, and focus on what I can hear or see or feel as a distraction. It's working.

I'm also working on turning the negative connotations associated with my symptoms into something more positive. When telling doctors and friends about my tinnitus symptoms, I usually labeled them as Radio Broadcast, Trains Come-a-Roaring, Wind Through the Cave in a Storm and Coach's Whistle.

Now that I've changed their labels, it has fundamentally changed how I deal with and react to them. Radio Broadcast is now called Communication From My Ancestors. Trains Come-a-Roaring is now referred to as Mark's Funky Bass Line. Wind Through the Cave in a Storm is now labeled Female Moans in the Midst of Orgasm. The Coach's Whistle is now a reminder of how lucky I am and how great life is. I call that one the Game Show Winning Buzzer these days. I go into the Game Show room, move my neck to the right, BUZZ! I'm reminded that I'm winning! BUZZ! I'm lucky! BUZZ! I will get through this! BUZZ! I can do this!

Dear Steve,

Your mind is your most powerful weapon. Your sword of truth. The beast is slain first through your belief that you can slay it. If you can change your thinking, change your outlook, anything is possible. You will get the results you desire, but the change in thinking is the first step. Steve, you need to believe that the implant is going to work when you start it up again next month, and that you will be able to adapt and evolve throughout the transition. It's your choice whether to believe that it will work or that it will fail. When you choose the positive, when you see through childlike eyes, when you focus your energy, when you see that anything is possible, you'll realize that everything is available to you. You can do it.

I love you, man,
Steve

Epilogue

It's been two years since I reactivated the implant. The flood is still there in all its variations, but I only notice them when I go to their rooms and visit them. Otherwise, I've completely blocked them out of my life. I can even write and talk about the flood without hearing the sounds or letting them distract me. I talked to my audiologist recently about all the noises in the flood, giving her detailed descriptions, for her data, and it had no effect on me. I don't give them any credit or recognize them anymore as a part of me. I decided, "I don't have the symptoms accompanied with tinnitus anymore."

Captain Kirk, as always, was right. "Focus on what you CAN hear" — or touch, smell, see or think. The implant definitely helped with this. It introduced new stimuli for my brain to focus on. Training my brain to understand what these stimuli mean gave me both the focus and distraction necessary to lock the doors on the flood noises. The surgery and implant activation — or more likely the combination of those two things and the diuretic drug — caused this flood, and then the implant helped me recover from it. One of many of life's conundrums. Probably not the last I'll deal with, but hopefully the heaviest. It definitely changed the way I see the world now. More power to me, right? If it doesn't kill you, it makes you stronger.

For 40 years, my brain had been gradually adjusting and accommodating to each stage of the hearing loss. At the time just before the cochlear implant surgery, I was peaked out and overprocessing every possible sound, vibration, sight and smell to accommodate for the deafness — working overtime trying to process these minute senses as "hearing." My brain was working 24 hours a day, seven days a week. Even when sleeping I would wake to the faintest vibration in the house. Then, when we activated the implant, the brain just overloaded. My brain didn't know what to do with this stimuli that it perceived as a foreign entity. The stimuli was overprocessed, overly identified, overattended to and reevaluated, and it just overwhelmed my brain and normal day-to-day functioning and processing of information.

As with the tinnitus storm, for almost 18 months, every thought I had was related to the sounds in my head. Then, when we activated the implant, there was this sudden new influx of stimuli, directly to my brain, which again dominated every thought, every second. Additionally, the level at which this stimuli entered was at decibel levels that have not been accepted by my brain for 30 years, and elevated the hyperacusis.

It took two years of training for my brain to finally shift back down to normal processing and functioning. Two years of slowly training the brain with one or two sounds a day. Like the doctors said, I had to keep it on and power through many situations these two years to break ground. Oftentimes, during this training, I would be in an overwhelming situation in which my brain was overloading from stimuli. Tracey and I would discuss that it's overloading, and we would go to the support plan instead of running and hiding. The last line of support for me before flight was to try to use the "white noise loop" app on my phone as a buffer. The white noise loop became my main support, and I still use it often. When there is overload, the white noise acts as a blanket over all the commotion and stimuli. It dampens the overload. It also works as a distraction for people suffering with tinnitus symptoms. It gives the brain something to focus on other than all the buzzing and hissing. The audiology community calls this strategy "masking."

One big issue associated with my implant was quiet times. The implant seems to make a mechanical shift when there's no noise around, through its "compression" settings. For example, if I'm sitting on the couch working on the laptop for two hours, home

220

alone, the implant would seem to shift itself higher, looking for sound. Then when actual sound enters, like the kids coming home, with doors banging and feet stomping, the implant projects this stimuli, or the brain receives this stimuli, in what seems to be a heightened and elevated level.

The white noise helps this problem too. When all is quiet, I can use the white noise to give the implant and brain something to focus on. Give the auditory processes of the brain some minor work to do until some real noises enter. The app offers a whole palette of noises, and I found that "pink noise" seems to work the best for me. Providing a warm blanket, matching, masking and distracting the tinnitus sounds, and exercising my brain during the quiet times.

Recently, I was watching the presidential debates, with closed captions, on my laptop and preparing dinner. I had to pick up my son from an activity and was disappointed that I would miss the next couple of responses. I took the Prius, because it is a quiet vehicle, and tried the radio to see if I could catch a word or two. Maybe two words together and just stay in the loop until I got back home. I cranked it up and was astonished that I was listening to the debates on the radio and understanding about 80 percent of the sentences! I pulled over and just sat for a few minutes listening to people talking on the radio! I realize that this is a controlled setting, with one person speaking at a time, and I know the context, but it's been 35 years since I understood a voice on the radio. It was shocking!

So now, during my commute, I train by alternating between talk radio for speech recognition and listening to bands like The Police for music recognition. Bands like The Police are good for my training because I'm very familiar with their music, they have a small group with just 3 instruments, and they're relatively clean in the sense that they don't use too many effects on their instruments.

Unfortunately, playing music, instrumental cognition and any kind of music writing straight-out disappeared after activation. I knew it would after the first activation of the implant, before the flood. I knew it would be a tradeoff for better communication, but it still sucked. When I tried to play a guitar, it sounded like "click, click, click-click." The implant picks up the physical hit of the pick against the strings. That's what it's programmed to do. Bring in those sounds that help with speech recognition. "Sss," "Fff," "Th," "Kk" —all those sounds that give differentiation to speech and help distinguish phonemes. It was immensely frustrating to have a guitar in my hand and not be able to connect it to my thoughts anymore, so I shut it down and put it in the back of the closet for the past two years.

Frequently, over those two years, I found myself telling students and friends that "I used to be a musician." But what if I still am? Recently, as the communication piece has started to level out, I've been thinking a little more positively. I've always been able to figure things out, so maybe I can retrain my brain to comprehend music this new way. Stata-ten, you understand?

Meanwhile, I'm hearing and comprehending all sorts of new environmental sounds every day. The gas pump talked to me recently. So did the crosswalk sign pole telling me to "Cross the street now." Shocking! Everything beeps and clicks these days. The crosswalk buttons, the stove buttons, controls in the car, assorted beeps and shweeps at the checkout line at the grocery store, bank machine buttons, the gas pump buttons, the washing machine ... and everybody's phones!

Communication has improved a hundredfold. I'm communicating with my family, people in stores and streets, and peers at work. I'm communicating using my voice and implant with my hearing students every day without much of a hassle. I drive my son to school and we talk a whole lot in the car, and sometimes I don't need to read his lips through the rearview mirror. I talk to my wife, on separate couches, and sometimes I look away and understand whole sentences. I'm hearing birds and crickets. I can hear the blinker clicking when I put on the turn signal. I am hearing the rain. I can hear the cat's meow. I am hearing the creek flow at the park. I can hear the wind in the trees. I can hear my daughter's voice.

"A baby's cry, a woman's sigh, a child's why, the long goodbye."

Afterword

My younger brother, Steve, recently wrote this book chronicling his hearing journey; specifically his journey becoming deaf and working with that challenge over the past 40 years. The book surprised me in so many ways because it taught me so much about Steve as a person—as my brother and as a man—and his perseverance inspired me. It also helped me see myself a bit differently and will likely do the same for other readers, which is why I want to articulate what I've learned and gained through reading it.

The book describes how my brother experienced situations throughout his life and how his hearing situation posed challenges (in some cases *small* and in some cases *huge*). At the end of each chapter, he wrote a letter to himself ("Dear Steve....") to take responsibility for his experience so that he fully owned it; being a *victor* and not a *victim*.

The book also brought back a lot of good memories of growing up, of family, friends and what life was like in high school and college. It was a fun read ... that's important. It was *fun*! I relished every chance to curl up somewhere and just spend some time with myself and Steve's book.

How do I see my brother in a different light? How did I get to know him as another person?

To start with, I got to see Steve as someone who works on himself and does his best to improve and grow. I can see that he works on himself on an internal level, and what is really special is the fact that he's doing it on his own. He doesn't have a group, teacher, tour guide or school that he's part of or where he draws guidance. He is self-driven.

Much of what he shares is very vulnerable and raw. He can open up his heart and shine a light on the hard stuff and bring it into the public eye—exposing a lot of his fears, anxieties, frustration, self-doubt and perceived shortcomings. Hence I see my brother as vulnerable, and I never really saw this aspect of him before.

I got to see Steve as a man—not as a kid, not a younger brother, not a lesser person (which usually goes along with being the younger brother). I got to see him as a man who takes responsibility for himself: his emotions, his choices, the cards he was dealt, the seed he was given. I am proud to see he is not a victim to his hearing challenges and works through each one in the best way he knows or discovers. I can see he is a leader of his own life. He is raising the type of family he wants as a committed husband and father, living where he wants. He's steering his teaching career as he sees fit while enjoying a very active social life. He is living his dream, not anyone else's, and to top it off, he is going for it, pushing his boundaries and not holding back when there is something he wants.

I see Steve as a success. He takes healthy risks and they are paying off for him.

I see Steve as a writer, as someone who can articulate, draw out from within, and use humor and storytelling to get thoughts and ideas out there that people can relate to and draw inspiration and strength from.

I see Steve as fun. Why? Because he is working at putting "fun" into his life. He is befriending himself in a positive way. He's rock climbing, running, building a wood-fired pizza oven, pursuing music, writing … all this and more, on top of having a family. He handles the negative stuff that comes up so it doesn't keep him down. In the book, he describes instances when he struggles with the concept of life not being fun and can slow himself down and recognize it and make choices to fix it.

The book also reminded me just how creative and talented my brother is. He has been a musician and recording artist all his life, despite the deafness, and has written and recorded at least 10 albums of original material, one of which is all children's songs. He wrote and produced a series of sign language movies, and I remembered his talent as a self-taught woodcarver crafting beautiful sculptures as well.

Steve can adapt and overcome. I got to see how through his hearing challenge. He chose to be creative, research, uncover solutions and sometimes just work around stuff. But the most important thing is he chose not to give up on himself.

I see how much Steve and I have in common. We both share a lot of the same challenges, workarounds and a similar underlying emotional matrix. As a person who has gone deaf, It was really interesting to see someone close to me experience some of the same issues, emotions, scars, healing and growth. I don't feel alone in what I've been experiencing. I am reminded too of how we all have our challenges, and we all must grow, change, let go, adapt.

I realize that all these positive qualities I discovered in my brother are a reflection of me and what I have inside. I must be able to see these things in myself first if I'm going to be able to see them in him. I'm reminded of how creative, successful, adaptable, articulate and fun I am. I am a leader of my own life and all that comes with it. I am living my dream and working hard to push it forward. I give my best and try to take responsibility for who I am.

Again, I am all these things I see in Steve, but for some reason, it's easier to see them in others sometimes … because often we're unwilling to recognize all the positive qualities in ourselves. But that's just how most people are—and I'm learning every day to further appreciate my gifts and just go for it.

Chris DiCesare

Steve DiCesare was born and raised in the suburbs of New York City. He currently lives in Colorado and teaches Special Education, ASL and Metalsmithing/Jewelry. Steve enjoys snowboarding and longboarding with the family, hiking and camping in the Rockies, and road trips in the pickup. When not driving the kids around, Steve might be found on a somewhat vertical lump of rock, fiercely attempting to safely solo navigate a blank slab of 5.5 choss.

Check out the Dear Steve, You're Going Deaf website at <u>youregoingdeaf.com</u> and Steve's music and video projects at <u>magoprojects.com</u>.

Ian Miller is a cartoonist, illustrator and part-time musician who was born and raised in New York but is now getting a head start on retirement in Florida. When he's not working on his beach body and fighting alligators, he's hard at work drawing. Since 2010 he has illustrated several graphic novels

and comic series, including the comic adaptation of the film Zombie With a Shotgun and the independent horror/fantasy series Something Real. In 2015 he became an official Wu-Tang Killa Bee by providing artwork for U-God's The Keynote Speaker album. You may also recognize his musical endeavors, but that's a story for another time.

Check out Ian's work at <u>ianjmiller.deviantart.com</u> and <u>Ianjmiller.com</u>